MW01602114

THE OCCIDENTAL QUARTERLY
Western Perspectives on Man, Culture, and Politics

THE OCCIDENTAL QUARTERLY: WESTERN PERSPECTIVES ON MAN, CULTURE, AND POLITICS (ISSN 1539-3925) is published by The Charles Martel Society four times yearly, in the Spring, Summer, Fall, and Winter. For information on subscriptions and back issues, see the inside of the back cover.

Editorial and Subscription Inquiries

THE OCCIDENTAL QUARTERLY
P. O. Box 8127
Atlanta, GA 31106 USA

Editor: EditorTOQ@theoccidentalquarterly.com
Reviews: Reviews@theoccidentalquarterly.com
Subscriptions: Subscribe@theoccidentalquarterly.com
Support: Support@theoccidentalquarterly.com

http://www.toqonline.com

Subscription and Back Issue Information
See the inside of the back cover.

VOL. 20, NO. 2   SUMMER 2020

TABLE OF CONTENTS

ARTICLES

REVIEW ESSAY

HEIDEGGER AND THE JEWISH QUESTION[1]

GREG JOHNSON

Martin Heidegger is one of the most celebrated and influential philosophers of the twentieth and now twenty-first centuries. Thus it is a problem that Heidegger was both a National Socialist and an anti-Semite, which are thought-crimes under the post-World War II intellectual dispensation.

The world has known that Heidegger was a National Socialist since 1933, but until recently, his precise attitude towards Jews was somewhat mysterious. Toni Cassirer, the wife of Jewish philosopher Ernst Cassirer, claimed in her autobiography that the Cassirers were aware that Heidegger was anti-Semitic in the late 1920s.[2]

However, whatever Heidegger's attitudes toward Jews were at the time, they were not impediments to carrying on extramarital affairs with Hannah Arendt, who was Jewish, and Elisabeth Blochmann, who was half-Jewish, or having cordial and mentoring relationships with Jewish teachers, students, and colleagues.[3]

During the Third Reich, Heidegger became Rector of the University of Freiburg, helping to purge the institution of Jewish students and faculty, although he protested against more vulgar manifestations of anti-Semitism and protested the sacking of certain Jewish faculty because it would make Germany look bad on the international stage.[4]

On June 30, 1933, after he had become Rector, Heidegger visited Karl Jaspers and his Jewish wife in Heidelberg. According to Jaspers, when he dismissed the *Protocols of the Learned Elders of Zion* as a forgery, Heidegger replied, "Nonetheless, there is a dangerous international alliance of Jews."[5]

---

[1] Based on a lecture at the inaugural meeting of the Scandza Forum in Stockholm on May 20, 2017.

[2] Toni Cassirer, *Mein Leben mit Ernst Cassirer* (Darmstadt: Wissenschaftliche Buchgesellschaft, 2003), 187.

[3] See Richard Wolin, *Heidegger's Children: Hannah Arendt, Karl Löwith, Hans Jonas, and Herbert Marcuse,* second ed. (Princeton: Princeton University Press, 2015).

[4] The best overall account of Heidegger and the Rectorate is still Hugo Ott's *Martin Heidegger: A Political Life* (New York: Basic Books, 1993).

[5] Quoted in Thomas Sheehan, "'Everyone Has to Tell the Truth': Heidegger and the Jews," *Continuum* 1, no. 1 (1990), 35, quoting and translating Karl Jaspers, *Philosophische Autobiographie*, expanded edition (Munich: Piper, 1977), 101.

Heidegger was right of course to dismiss the "forgery" canard. The *Protocols*, like the dialogues of Plato, are a literary presentation of ideas whose truth depends on their correspondence with reality. It is thus simply irrelevant to protest that they are not really verbatim transcripts of actual conversations.

After the war, Heidegger was forced to undergo de-Nazification. He was characterized as a Nazi fellow-traveler and banned from teaching until 1951. Heidegger enraged Jews by refusing to treat the holocaust as a morally and metaphysically unique event. Instead he compared it to other wartime atrocities and claimed that it had to be understood as a manifestation of the modern mindset that sees all of reality as material for human manipulation and control.[6] Also controversial was his decision in 1953 to publish a 1935 lecture course, *Introduction to Metaphysics*, in which he characterized "the inner truth and greatness" of the National Socialist movement as "the encounter between global technology and modern humanity."[7]

New light was thrown on Heidegger's attitudes toward Jews beginning in his centennial year of 1989, when Heidegger's *Contributions to Philosophy (Of the Event)*, was published posthumously. *Contributions* focuses on the central concept of Heidegger's later thinking, the "*Ereignis*" or event of appropriation, which is Heidegger's term for how fundamental historical changes in the realm of meaning take place. *Contributions* was written between 1936 and 1938, at the time that Heidegger was lecturing extensively on Nietzsche and articulating his dissent from National Socialist orthodoxy. But it was still quite surprising to find Heidegger agreeing with the orthodox National Socialist claim "Bolshevism is in fact Jewish" in the *Contributions*, even though Heidegger gave very different reasons, arguing that Bolshevism is Jewish because Bolshevism is an offshoot of Christian egalitarianism, and Christianity is an offshoot of Judaism.[8]

Also published in 1989 was a 1929 letter from Heidegger to Victor Schwoerer, the vice-president of the Notgemeinschaft der Deutschen

---

[6] Alan Milchman and Alan Rosenberg, *Martin Heidegger and the Holocaust* (Buffalo, NY: Prometheus Books, 1997) and Mahon O'Brien, *Heidegger, History, and the Holocaust* (New York: Bloomsbury, 2017).

[7] See part 4 of Collin Cleary, "Heidegger: An Introduction for Anti-Moderns," in his *What is a Rune? & Other Essays*, Greg Johnson (ed.) (San Francisco: Counter-Currents, 2015).

[8] Martin Heidegger, *Gesamtausgabe* [Complete Works], vol. 65, *Beiträge zur Philosophie (Vom Ereignis)*, ed. Friedrich-Wilhelm von Herrmann (Frankfurt am Main: Vittorio Klostermann, 1989), 54. In English: Martin Heidegger, *Contributions to Philosophy (Of the Event)*, trans. Richard Rojcewicz and Daniela Vallega-Neu (Bloomington: Indiana University Press, 2012), 44.

Wissenschaft. In the letter, Heidegger spoke of the necessity of promoting talented German scholars in order to combat the "Jewification" (*Verjudung*) of German intellectual life.[9] In 2005 a line from a letter from Heidegger to his wife Elfride, dated October 18, 1918, came to light. Heidegger wrote, "The Jewification of our culture and universities is certainly horrifying, and I think that the German race really should summon up the inner strength to find its feet again."[10]

These two letters clearly indicate that Heidegger opposed increasing Jewish influence on German cultural life almost fifteen years before Hitler's rise to power, and more than a decade later not only did his attitude remain unchanged, he was taking active steps to combat Jewish power. His desire to see the "German race" fight back against Jewish influence and his willingness to actually cultivate and promote German scholars to counter Jewish influence explains his enthusiasm for National Socialism and his willingness to help implement National Socialist policies at the University of Freiburg.

However, in the Winter Semester of 1932–1933, before Heidegger openly embraced the party and became Rector at Freiburg, he wrote a letter to Hannah Arendt about rumors that he was an anti-Semite. After detailing all the favors he was doing for Jews during his sabbatical, he wrote:

> Whoever wants to call that "raging anti-Semitism" is welcome to do so. Beyond that, I am now just as much an anti-Semite in university issues as I was ten years ago in Marburg, where, because of this anti-Semitism, I even earned Jacobsthal's and Friedländer's support. To say absolutely nothing about my personal relationships with Jews (e.g., Husserl, Misch, Cassirer, and others). And above all, it cannot touch my relationship to you.[11]

Heidegger's claim that he is "just as much an anti-Semite in university issues as I was ten years ago" was meant to be taken as sarcasm by Arendt, implying that he was not an anti-Semite then or now. Why else would he cite the support of two Jewish colleagues, archaeologist Paul Jacobsthal and

---

[9] See Ulrich Sieg, "Die Verjudung des deutschen Geistes. Ein unbekannter Brief Heideggers," *Die Zeit* 52 (December 22, 1989).

[10] Martin Heidegger, *Letters to his Wife, 1915–1970*, ed. Gertrud Heidegger, trans. R. D. V. Glasgow (Cambridge: Polity Press, 2008), 28.

[11] Hannah Arendt and Martin Heidegger, *Letters, 1925–1975*, ed. Ursula Ludz, trans. Andrew Shields (New York: Harcourt, 2004), 52–53. This letter was first published in 1998.

classicist Paul Friedländer? But another reading is possible: The statement could also be taken at face value. Heidegger really was anti-Semitic with regard to university issues in Marburg and in Freiburg, as would soon become clear. Heidegger had merely *concealed* his anti-Semitism from his colleagues—as he was concealing it from Arendt herself in this very letter. But when Hitler came to power, dissimulation was no longer necessary. Arendt herself certainly felt deceived. In later years, she declared that "Heidegger was notorious for lying about everything."[12]

Beginning in 2014, a flood of new light on Heidegger and the Jews was cast by the publication of the first three volumes of Heidegger's *Black Notebooks* (*Gesamtausgabe*; hereafter *GA*).[13] A fourth volume appeared in 2015.[14] These volumes encompass writings from 1931 to 1948. Jews and Judaism are mentioned in only 25 places in the 1,753 pages of the *Black Notebooks* published so far—fewer than ten pages, if we are generous in providing context—beginning in 1938 and ending *circa* 1948. In the following, I will use Richard Polt's "References to Jews and Judaism in Martin Heidegger's *Black Notebooks*, 1938–1948" as a source for translations of these passages.[15]

But in Heidegger scholarship—as in politics, culture, and academia at large—the Jewish tail wags the dog. Thus the question of Heidegger and the Jews has become the topic of a flurry academic conferences, articles, and books, as well as articles in the middlebrow press.[16] These discussions are filled with the language of contamination and contagion. Anti-Semitism is treated as an intellectual form of lice or typhus, and scholars earnestly debate whether they or their students can catch cooties from reading

---

[12] Elisabeth Young-Bruehl, *Hannah Arendt: For Love of the World* (New Haven: Yale University Press, 1982), 247.

[13] Martin Heidegger, *Gesamtausgabe*, vol. 94, *Überlegungen* [Ponderings] *II–VI*, ed. Peter Trawny (Frankfurt am Main: Vittorio Klostermann, 2014), *Gesamtausgabe*, vol. 95, *Überlegungen VII–XI*, ed. Peter Trawny (Frankfurt am Main: Vittorio Klostermann, 2014), and *Gesamtausgabe*, vol. 96, *Überlegungen XII–XV*, ed. Peter Trawny (Frankfurt am Main: Vittorio Klostermann, 2014).

[14] Martin Heidegger, *Gesamtausgabe*, 97 *Anmerkungen* [Notes] *I–V*, ed. Peter Trawny (Frankfurt am Main: Vittorio Klostermann, 2015).

[15] Richard Polt, "References to Jews and Judaism in Martin Heidegger's *Black Notebooks*, 1938–1948," Unpublished ms, Academia.edu (November, 2017).

https://www.academia.edu/11943010/References_to_Jews_and_Judaism_in_Martin_Heidegger_s_Black_Notebooks_1938-1948

Polt translates 25 passages from *The Black Notebooks* and an additional passage from *The History of Beyng*.

[16] See Andrzej Serafin, "A Reception History of the *Black Notebooks*," *Gatherings: The Heidegger Circle Annual*, vol. 5, *Heidegger's Black Notebooks* (2015),

http://www.heideggercircle.org/Gatherings2015-06Serafin.pdf

Heidegger. When the hubbub about anti-Semitism dies down, however, I think the world of letters will eventually conclude that the *Black Notebooks* is one of Heidegger's richest and most compelling publications.

Indeed, I suspect that Heidegger, his family, and Vittorio Klostermann, his publishing house, handled the publication and promotion of the *Black Notebooks* in a quite cunning manner. Heidegger surely knew that these volumes would be highly controversial, so he specified that they be published last in his collected works—like an unexpected verb at the end of a long, meandering German sentence that suddenly charges everything that came before with new meaning and life. If there was going to be a controversy about Heidegger and anti-Semitism, best to wait until Heidegger scholars were maximally invested in his work. Moreover, the decision to leak the most inflammatory passages on Jews before the publication of the *Black Notebooks* was a masterstroke of marketing, for the predictable controversy in the press made the *Black Notebooks* philosophical best-sellers.

In 2016, excepts from Heidegger's correspondence with his brother Fritz dealing with National Socialism, World War II, and related topics were published. A similar wag-the-dog phenomenon can be observed in this publication. Although the letters make only passing and anodyne references to Jews, they were published as *Martin Heidegger und der Antisemitismus*.[17] The volume is co-edited by rabbi Walter Homolka and Arnulf Heidegger, one of Martin Heidegger's grandsons. The book contains 127 pages of letters and 262 pages of scholarly essays on Heidegger and anti-Semitism.

So what do the *Black Notebooks* say about Jews? Heidegger's remarks fall into four broad categories. Sixteen of the 25 references refer to Jewish intellectuals and movements, certain Jewish individuals, and Judaism as a religion. The remaining nine refer to Jews as a nation.

JEWISH INTELLECTUALS AND MOVEMENTS

In discussing doctrines of human nature, Heidegger refers to the "Christian-Jewish doctrine . . . that define[s] man immediately on the basis of his relation to a 'God' . . ." (1938; *GA* 94: 475–76). Elsewhere, Heidegger speaks of rejecting the "*anthropological* determination of man, and with it, all previous anthropology—Christian Hellenistic-Jewish and Socratic-Platonic" (1938–1939; *GA* 95: 322). Heidegger also wonders if thinking of human beings as a people (*volk*) tacitly accepts the "Hellenistic-Jewish 'world,'" i.e.,

---

[17] Walter Homolka and Arnulf Heidegger, eds., *Heidegger und der Antisemitismus: Positionen in Widerstreit. Mit briefen von Martin und Fritz Heidegger* (Freiburg im Breisgau: Herder, 2016).

worldview, that he wishes to question and transcend (1938–1939; *GA* 95: 339).

There is nothing specifically anti-Semitic about these references to intellectual traditions. Heidegger rejects Jewish thinking, but he does not single it out. He hyphenates Jewish ideas with Christianity and Hellenistic thought and places these hyphenated constructs on a par with Socratic-Platonic thinking, which he also rejects. Moreover, it is not really anti-Semitic to reject Jewish ideas if one thinks they are false. It would only be anti-Semitic if one rejected them simply because they are Jewish, and obviously that is not what Heidegger is doing here.

In a remark on the *völkisch* outlook, Heidegger asks, "Is it an accident that National Socialism has stamped out 'sociology' as a term? Why was sociology gladly pursued by Jews and Catholics?" (1938–1939; *GA* 95: 161). There is nothing specifically anti-Semitic about this remark either. Heidegger is not singling out Jews but placing them alongside Catholics. Heidegger's likely answer to the question he raises is that both Jews and the Catholic church are international rather than national communities, thus they are attracted to sociology as a universal science.

In a remark on his critique of Cartesianism in *Being and Time*, Heidegger mentions that "it has been exploited just as strongly by Jews as by National Socialists, without being grasped in its essential core . . ." (1938–1939; *GA* 95: 168–69). Again, there is nothing anti-Semitic about this remark. Heidegger is putting some Jews and some National Socialists on the same plane, as having a superficial understanding of his critique of Cartesianism, although he may well be implying that their being Jewish contributed to their superficial understanding.

In a remark on self-knowledge, Heidegger argues that the very idea of self-reflection is superficial, "even after one has pushed Jewish 'psychoanalysis' aside" (1938–1939; *GA* 95: 258). Again, there is nothing specifically anti-Semitic about this remark, although, like many intellectuals of the period, he was identifying psychoanalysis as a Jewish movement, as indeed it is. Heidegger's point is that National Socialist critics of "Jewish 'psychoanalysis'" fail to question the idea of self-reflection and thus end up on the same plane.

Heidegger makes a similar point elsewhere, mentioning Freud by name:

One should not get all too loudly indignant about the psychoanalysis of the Jew "Freud" if, and as long as, one cannot *at all* "think" about each and every thing other than by "tracing" everything as an "expression" of "life" back to "instincts" and "the atrophy of instinct."

This way of "thinking," which in advance excludes all "being" whatsoever, is pure nihilism. (*circa* 1941; *GA* 96: 218)

Here Heidegger is again criticizing National Socialist thinkers who indignantly condemn "the Jew 'Freud'" yet themselves reduce psychology to instincts.

I think it is reasonable to read Heidegger's very National Socialist-sounding use of the phrase "the Jew 'Freud'" as sarcastic echoing of National Socialist cant.[18] This is reinforced by putting Freud's name in scare quotes, which may mean that Heidegger believes the unnamed National Socialist writers are attacking a straw man, not Freud's actual teachings.

In a reflection on "dogmatism, be it ecclesiastical-political or state-political," Heidegger observes the tendency of the authorities to attribute any dissent from dogma as the work of "*the enemy* for it (for the dogmatism) — be it the heathens and godless ones, or the Jews and communists." Given that "the Jews and communists" are the enemies, the dogma in question is clearly National Socialism. What's more, Heidegger identifies himself with the dissidents, not the dogmatists.

MENTIONS OF JEWISH INDIVIDUALS

In addition to Freud, Heidegger mentions several other Jewish individuals in the *Black Notebooks*.

In one passage Heidegger mentions two Jewish swindlers, Iwan Baruch Kutisker and Julius Barmat, who, according to the National Socialists, epitomized the Weimar Republic:

What is the difference between the following occurrences? Barmat and Kutisker make good business for themselves out of the postwar democracy; with the help of the National Socialist world view, primary school teachers turn into "philosophers" with whom a serious person would never bother. There is no difference; for in the latter case the historical essence of National Socialism is grasped as little as is, in the former case, the historical essence of parliamentary democracy. (1941; *GA* 96: 234).

---

[18] Heidegger spoke of "the Jew Fränkel" in a manner that cannot be interpreted as sarcastic in a report written in 1933 to stab Eduard Baumgarten, a former colleague, in the back. The report was ignored because it was so obviously written out of hatred. See Victor Farías, *Heidegger and Nazism*, ed. Joseph Margolis and Tom Rockmore (Philadelphia: Temple University Press, 1989), 210.

Here Heidegger is saying that two Jewish swindlers no more reveal the essence of parliamentary democracy than unnamed German academic frauds reveal the essence of National Socialism. This is actually a critique of National Socialist propaganda and a refutation of an argument against liberal democracy, although it also amounts to an analogous defense of National Socialism.

In another passage, Heidegger writes, "At the same time, the 'cunning' of Bolshevist politics comes to light. The Jew Litvinov surfaces again." (June, 1941; *GA* 96: 242). This may well be an unironic use of the National Socialist trope.

JUDAISM AS A RELIGION

In a remark on Karl Barth, Heidegger writes, "The Phariseeism of Karl Barth and his associates exceeds even the ancient Jewish Phariseeism, by the degree that is necessarily posited by the modern history of being" (*GA* 95: 395–96; 1938–1939). Here again, no anti-Semitic judgment is intended. Indeed, Heidegger puts the Jewish Pharisees on a higher rung than a German Christian theologian.

Heidegger mentions Judaism in a number of post-war reflections from 1946 to 1948. Around 1946 he writes:

> "Prophecy" is the technique for fending off what is destinal in history. It is an instrument of the will to power. That the great prophets are Jews is a fact whose secret has not yet been thought through. (Note for jackasses: this comment has nothing to do with "anti-Semitism," which is as foolish and abominable as Christianity's bloody and, above all, non-bloody attacks on "heathens." The fact that Christianity even brands anti-Semitism as "un-Christian" is part of its highly developed and refined power technique.) (*GA* 97: 159)

In this passage, Heidegger himself denies anti-Semitic intent or import. While his comment on the Jews places them in a class by themselves, his comment on anti-Semitism places it in the same company as the Church's anti-heathenism, which Heidegger clearly rejects. Of course, he is only speaking here of Christian religious anti-Semitism, which leaves open the door to other types.

In 1947 or 1948, Heidegger writes, "God is the God of Abraham, the God of Jesus. But there is no God of be-ing" (*GA* 97: 357). A few pages later we read, "*On the doctrine of gods.* — Jehovah is the god who presumed to make himself the chosen god, and not to tolerate any other gods beside himself."

(*GA* 97: 369). And a few pages after that, we find:

> What if the god of the philosophers were still more divine than the god of Abraham, who tolerated no others of his kind aside from himself, and whose son Jesus sent all who did not love him to Hell and let them roast there? What sort of god is it who denies divinity, and who has none of the generosity of pure joy at his kind and at their inexhaustible richness? (A note on Pascal.) (*GA* 97: 409)

Finally, in a note from around 1948, Heidegger simply states, "The modern systems of total dictatorship stem from Judeo-Christian monotheism" (*GA* 97: 438).

None of these passages are specifically anti-Semitic. Indeed, they apply to Christianity as much as Judaism. The first alludes to Pascal, and the third mentions him by name. Heidegger is clearly critical of the Biblical God, but his remarks are no more anti-Jewish than anti-Christian. And the last remark is also as anti-National Socialist as it is anti-Judeo-Christian.

SOME PRELIMINARY CONCLUSIONS

Of the sixteen references to Jews and Judaism that we have examined thus far, only one might be patently anti-Semitic, namely "the Jew Litvinov."

There are six references to the Jewish or Judeo-Christian religion, one of which is explicitly anti-anti-Semitic, one of which places Jews above a German Christian, three of which are as much about Christianity as Judaism, and one of which is as anti-National Socialist as it is anti-Judeo-Christian.

Jews are mentioned alongside communists as enemies of the National Socialist state, which Heidegger is taking to task for state-political "dogmatism."

There are references to "Christian-Jewish," "Christian Hellenistic-Jewish," and "Hellenistic-Jewish" conceptions of human nature, the latter two of which Heidegger places on the same rung as the "Socratic-Platonic" conception.

Some Jews are placed on the same rung as some National Socialists in misunderstanding Heidegger's critique of Cartesianism. Other Jews are placed on the same rung as some Catholics in advocating the science of sociology. National Socialist psychologists are placed on the same rung as Freud because they too embrace self-reflection as a model of knowledge and instincts as an explanation of psychological states. Even the Jewish swindlers Barmat and Kutisker are placed on the same level as unnamed

National Socialist educational careerists.

A clear pattern is developing here. In twelve out of sixteen passages, Heidegger places Jews, Judaism, and Jewish thought on the same level as Christianity, the Greeks, and German National Socialists. In all these cases, Heidegger rejects the Jewish as well as the non-Jewish terms as equally problematic. In the passages where Heidegger places Jews and National Socialists on the same plane, his primary target is National Socialists, for whom the cruelest barb is to be compared to Jews. But Heidegger's problem with the Jews is not that they are Jews, but that their ideas are as false and superficial as their National Socialist counterparts.

With these patterns in mind, we will now examine Heidegger's remarks on Jews as a people.

JEWS AS A PEOPLE

Heidegger discusses "Jewry" (*Judentum, Judenschaft*), meaning Jews as a people, in nine places in the *Black Notebooks*. I will also discuss a tenth reference to Jews as a people that was discovered in the manuscript called *Die Geschichte des Seyns* (*The History of Beyng*, 1938–40) and published in 2014. All of these passages are anti-Semitic in an unproblematic fashion. They fall into three rough categories: descriptions of Jewish misbehavior, explanations of Jewish misbehavior, and remarks on fighting against Jewry.

Four passages fall into the first category.

1.

One of the most secret forms of the *gigantic*, and perhaps the oldest, is the tenacious skillfulness in calculating, hustling, and intermingling through which the worldlessness of Jewry is grounded. (1938–1939; *GA* 95: 97)

Here Heidegger remarks on how diaspora Jewry, because of its rootlessness and predominantly commercial form of life is uniquely adapted to the conditions of modernity, which Heidegger characterizes by "worldlessness" and "the gigantic." (*das Riesige*). Heidegger believes that both meaning and measure are endowed by rootedness in a particular language, culture, and homeland. Rootlessness, therefore, leads to worldlessness (a void of meaning) and the gigantic (an abolition of limits; bigger is always better; new is always improved). Both worldlessness and the gigantic are forms of nihilism that are characteristic of modernity.

2.

World Jewry, incited by emigrants allowed to leave Germany, is pervasive and impalpable, and even though its power is widespread, it doesn't need to participate in military actions, whereas all that remains to us is to sacrifice the best blood of our own people. (*circa* September 1941; *GA* 96: 262; my trans.)

In this passage, Heidegger expresses the belief that diaspora Jewry, stirred up by Jews forced out of Germany by the National Socialists, are responsible for the strange alliance of Soviet communists and Anglo-Saxon capitalists fighting against Germany. Furthermore, Heidegger remarks that Jews are warmongers, masterfully inciting gentiles to fight their battles for them.

3.

Through this "history," the essence of history comes to the brink of a decision, for the first time, between *nothing and be-ing* — the imperialistic-bellicose way of thinking and the humanistic-pacifist way of thinking are only "dispositions" that belong to each other, each brought forward in different ways as a pretext, "historiological" — "history"-making "dispositions" in whose realms no decisions are possible anymore — because they are just offshoots of "metaphysics."

Thus both can be used by "international Jewry" to proclaim and accomplish one as a means for the other — this machinational "history" — making entangles all players equally in their webs (*circa* 1940; *GA* 96: 133; my trans.)

In the first paragraph of this passage, Heidegger alludes to an idea that recurs in some of his other remarks about National Socialism and Jewry. Heidegger had hoped that National Socialism heralded a fundamental turning point in Western civilization, which he here characterizes as a decision between "*nothing and be-ing*," which is really the most fundamental choice of all.

For Heidegger, it was a choice between cosmopolitan rootlessness, unbounded nihilism, and the conquest of nature versus rootedness in culture, tradition, and homelands; an acceptance of finitude and uncertainty; and a sense that we are part of the natural world, charged with being its guardians, not its exploiters and consumers.

Heidegger, however, was deeply disappointed in National Socialism. As the Third Reich unfolded, he came to see it as just another form of modern technological civilization, fighting over much smaller stakes, like the difference between imperialism and pacificism. Heidegger saw these as merely alternatives *within* modernity, whereas he was hoping for an alternative *to* modernity. As he puts it, imperialism and pacifism are both "just offshoots of 'metaphysics,'" by which Heidegger means the Western tradition from Plato to Nietzsche, the outcome of which is the modern technological nihilism that he hoped National Socialism would go beyond.

Heidegger does not, however, think that the metaphysical ideas of thinkers like Plato and Nietzsche are actually the *causes* of the modern world. Heidegger does not think that philosophers and poets are the "unacknowledged legislators of mankind," who create the blueprints according to which history is built. Instead, Heidegger thinks that philosophers and poets are merely the first people attuned to changes in history and culture that cannot be meaningfully reduced to human intentions and purposeful activity and are fundamentally mysterious and unpredictable. For Heidegger, philosophy is not "behind" historical change; historical change is "behind" philosophy. Moreover, Heidegger believed that we cannot get "behind" historical change. It cannot be explained. It just happens. The idea that the human mind is behind historical change is sometimes called "humanism." Heidegger's idea that historical change is behind the human mind is thus referred to as his "anti-humanism."

This explains the distinction in the passage above between history and "history" in quotes. When Heidegger uses history without quotes, he is referring to his own anti-humanist conception of history. When Heidegger places history in quotes, he is referring to the humanist conception of history as something that human beings create according to blueprints that they think up. The idea that mankind can make history according to our designs is just another manifestation of technological nihilism, which in the *Black Notebooks* Heidegger calls "machination" (*Machenschaft*), which connotes plans and schemes as well as technological manipulation and control.

The fact that human beings cannot really make history does not, of course, prevent them from *trying*. The unfolding political and environmental catastrophes of the twentieth and twenty-first centuries are all exercises in what Heidegger calls "machinational 'history'-making." But Heidegger claims that the very idea that mankind can understand and control everything is not something that we can understand and control. We don't understand why we think we can understand everything. We can't control the idea that we can control everything. The idea that human reason makes us masters of the world is, ironically, a groundless mania that enthralls us. Machinational "history"-making is an inscrutable dispensation from what Heidegger here calls the "decision regions" of genuine history. To speak of decision in this context, however, is misleading, because there is no subject or will behind history. It is a decision without a decider.

All those who fight over issues framed within the context of modernity—Jew and German alike—are equally entangled in its web. But because "international Jewry"—Heidegger himself puts the words in quotes, which indicates a reluctance to make the phrase his own—is a rootless and calculating people, it is uniquely adapted to modernity. Thus Jews are equally capable of using imperialism and pacifism as means to their ends in the struggle for power. Jews, moreover, have a systematic advantage over Germans and other rooted peoples in struggling for power within the context of global technological nihilism.

In the *Black Notebooks* and contemporary writings, Heidegger characterizes the outcome of machinational "history"-making as "global criminality" (*Verbrechen*). In 1941, he declared that:

> The authentic experience that has been allotted to today's generation, but which it was not able to take over, see through, and lay back into its essential inception, is the unrestricted outbreak of the unconditioned criminality of the modern human essence, in accordance with its role in the empowerment of power into machination. Criminality [*Verbrechen*]: that is no mere breaking up [*Zerbrechen*], but the devastation of everything into what is broken. (1941; *GA* 96: 266)

This provides the context for passage number 4, from the manuscript of *The History of Beyng*:

4.

One would need to ask in what the peculiar predetermination of Jewry [*Judenschaft*] for global criminality is grounded. (Quoted in Peter Trawny, *Heidegger und der Mythos der jüdischen Weltverschwörung* [Frankfurt am Main: Vittorio Klostermann, 2014], p. 51)

Heidegger treats it as a matter of fact that Jews have a marked predisposition for global criminality. But as a philosopher, he cannot be comfortable merely noting this fact. He wants to understand it, which is the subject of the next three passages.

All three of these passages touch upon the question of whether Jews are best understood as a biological race or as a nation. Heidegger is clearly skeptical that anything essential about Jewry can be understood in simple biological terms. For Heidegger, Jews are first and foremost a people, defined by a common cultural heritage and a common destiny that cannot be meaningfully reduced to or explained by biological race.

5.

Jewry's temporary increase in power is, however, grounded in the fact that Western metaphysics, especially in its modern development, furnishes the starting point for the diffusion of a generally empty rationality and calculative ability, which in this manner took up residence in the "spirit," without being able to grasp the hidden decision realms on its own. The more originary and primordial the prospective decisions and questions, the more they remain inaccessible to this "race."

In the first sentence above, Heidegger states straightforwardly that Jewry's "temporary increase in power" is grounded in the modern spirit of technical-instrumental rationality. Since Jews have long lived as a rootless, commercial diaspora people, they found themselves uniquely adapted to the spirit of the modern age and thus naturally rose to positions of power. Heidegger believes this power is "temporary," because he believed that modernity's days are numbered.

Jews are not, however, merely objects of the historical process. They are also agents. Modernity cleared the way for them, but their own will to dominate pushed them into positions of power, and once there, they used that power to push the modernization process further. Thus Jews as a people also bear responsibility for intensified globalization.

Heidegger's views should be contrasted to conspiratorial accounts of Jewish power like the *Protocols*. For Heidegger, the *Protocols* and other conspiratorial views of history are naïvely "humanistic." They presuppose that "machinational 'history'-making" really is possible. They posit that some human beings have the immense power and knowledge necessary to create history according to their own designs—whereas the vast majority of humanity has no power or responsibility in this area.

For Heidegger, however, the ultimate causes of historical change lie outside our powers of prediction and control. Thus Jews did not create the modern world as an exercise in machinational history-making. But because of their superior adaptation to modernity, they now enjoy more power and more responsibility than any other nation for the present unfolding of modernity.

Heidegger's claim that empty rationality and calculation have taken up residence in the realm of the "spirit" (a term Heidegger himself puts in quotes) and are unable to grasp the "hidden decision realms" is a reference to his idea that the modern conviction that we can understand and control everything is the product of historical forces that we can neither understand nor control, and which are thus invisible to the modern mind. Because Jews as a people are the vanguard of rootlessness and calculation, they are the least capable of grasping the hidden realm from which historical change emerges.

Heidegger then offers parenthetically an example of this Jewish blindness to the ultimate origins of historical change: his own mentor and the founder of phenomenology, Edmund Husserl.

(Thus Husserl's writing on phenomenological observation while dismissing psychological explanation and historical settlement of opinions is of lasting significance—and yet it goes nowhere near the regions of essential decisions, but rather presupposes the historical tradition of philosophy throughout; the necessary consequence is reflected immediately in the swing to neo-Kantian transcendental philosophy that eventually makes a progression to a Hegelianism in the formal sense inevitable. My "attack" against Husserl is not directed against him alone and indeed inessentially—my attack goes to the neglect of the question of Being, i.e., the essence of metaphysics as such, on the ground of which the machination of beings can determine history. The attack grounds a historical moment of the highest decision-making between the primacy of beings and the grounding of the truth of Be-ing.) (*circa* 1939; *GA* 96: 46; my trans.)

One has to ask, however, if Husserl, who was Jewish, was really any more blind to Heidegger's concerns than, say, Kant, who was German? At the end, Heidegger makes it clear that his objection is not to Husserl as a Jew, or Husserl specifically, but to the overall neglect of the question of Being, which in this context refers to the ultimate cause of historical change, and to philosophizing within the framework of the metaphysical tradition, which gives rise to modernity. Heidegger's attack on the metaphysical tradition is an attempt to find an alternative to modernity, a new beginning for Western man.

6.

The idea of an understanding with England in terms of a distribution of imperialist "prerogatives" misses the essence of the historical process, which is led by England within the framework of Americanism and Bolshevism and at the same time world Jewry to its final conclusion. The question of the role of world Jewry is not racial, but the metaphysical question of the type of humanity that can accept the world-historical "task" of uprooting all beings from Being. (*GA* 96: 243; my trans.)

Hitler admired the British Empire and wished to preserve it. Hitler also wanted to create an empire in Eastern Europe at the expense of Poland, Ukraine, and Russia. He hoped that Germany and Britain could reach an agreement not to fight with one another or interfere with one another's imperial projects. Thus in this passage, Heidegger is criticizing Hitler's thinking as superficial. As in passage number 3, above, Heidegger thinks that the struggle between empires, like the struggle between imperialism and pacifism, is superficial because it fails to understand that all of these options lie within the framework of modernity and are thus not alternatives to it.

For Heidegger, the "essence of the historical process" in modernity is the unbounded expansion of nihilism. In this passage, he speaks of "the world-historical 'task' of uprooting all beings from Being." For Heidegger, "Being" refers to the realm of meaning, thus "uprooting" beings from Being means uprooting them from the realm of meaning, and the loss of meaning is nihilism.

Heidegger sees both Bolshevism and Anglo-American capitalism as merely different forms of the same technological nihilism. For Heidegger, an understanding with Britain is not possible, since Britain was not merely opposed to Germany's imperialistic aims. Because Britain was an individualist, commercial-exploratory-imperialist seafaring civilization, she played a leading role in the global propagation of rootlessness and nihilism. Such a Britain could not allow a Germany that stood for rootedness, nationalism, and hierarchy and against globalization and leveling. Thus Britain used Hitler's invasion of Poland as the pretext to start World War II, and was central to creating the alliance between Anglo-American capitalism and Soviet communism against German National Socialism.

But Britain is not the only nation in the vanguard of nihilism. World Jewry exceeds even Britain in rootlessness, commercialism, and calculation. Thus of all nations, the Jews are the best adapted to the spirit of modernity to rise to a position of leadership. This is why Heidegger says that that "question of the role of world Jewry is not racial, but . . . metaphysical." Jews enjoy power and influence in modernity because of their long cultural adaptation to being a diaspora people and their collective will-to-power and sense they are destined for world rulership. Racial factors like IQ can't hurt, but they do not explain why Jews gravitated toward banking, the media, and culture-creation, while other market-dominant diaspora peoples gravitated toward cheap hotels and hardware stores. Jews are powerful because they are "the type of humanity that can accept the world-historical 'task' of uprooting all beings from Being." Jews then, really are a "chosen people" after all: "chosen" by the historical process to spread technological nihilism to the four corners of the earth.

7.

The Jews, *with their marked talent for calculation*, have "lived" longer than anyone by the principle of race, which is why they are resisting its consistent application with utmost violence. The establishment [*Einrichtung*] of racial breeding [eugenics] does not stem from "life" itself, but from the overpowering of life through machination. What it pushes forward with such a plan is the complete *deracialization* of all peoples by clamping them into a uniformly constructed and tailored establishment [*Einrichtung*] of all beings. At one with de-racialization is the self-alienation of peoples — the loss of history — i.e., the decision realms of Be-ing. (*circa* 1939; *GA* 96: 56; my trans.)

Here Heidegger observes a classic Jewish double standard. Jews have practiced racism and eugenics longer than any other nation, yet they oppose the racism and eugenics of other peoples. But Heidegger's main point is that eugenics is not a manifestation of the life force, but of the domination of life by modernity, i.e., by technological nihilism. But if eugenics is a manifestation of technological nihilism, then one cannot use eugenics to fight against it.

If eugenics really is a manifestation of technological nihilism, what does it lead to? Heidegger speaks of *uniformity* and *deracialization*, but he does not really explain them. Perhaps, though, we can understand them along the following lines. If people can choose the traits of their children, will they choose to make them more fit or less fit for functioning in the modern world? Clearly the tendency will be to make children more adapted to modernity. But modernity is rootless, globalized, calculating, and nihilistic. Thus any people that practices eugenics in the modern age will tend to deracialize itself and to converge toward the creation of a homogeneous global modern man. In other words, there will be a tendency to become more and more like Jews. Which means that eugenics is a form of nihilism, not an alternative to it. The better adapted we are to modernity, the further we are from understanding the sources of modernity and its alternatives, namely "the decision realms of Be-ing."

How, then, can we fight against technological nihilism without falling back into it? This is the topic of Heidegger's last three passages. As Heidegger's letters on resisting the "Jewification" of German life indicate, he was not merely interested in understanding Jewish power, he also wished to combat it. Heidegger wished, however, to counter Jewish power on the most fundamental level, namely by fighting against the rootless, nihilistic modern world in which Jewish power flourished and for a new beginning—a rooted, meaningful world in which Jewish power would wither. He wanted to drain the swamp in which the mosquitos flourish. Thus Heidegger constantly emphasizes the futility of fighting modern nihilism by means of modern nihilism.

8.

To appropriate "culture" as a means of power and thus to assert oneself and affect a superiority is at bottom *Jewish* behavior. What follows from this for *cultural politics* as such? (1938–1939; *GA* 95: 326)

Heidegger is referring here to at least three well-known Jewish phenomena. First, there is the *appropriation* of European culture by Jewish collectors, connoisseurs, performers, and scholars, which—regardless of any genuine appreciation—is regarded as a "means of power," i.e., a pathway of Jewish upward mobility, of self-assertion and a desire for superiority within the status system of gentile society.

Second, there is the Jewish *deconstruction* of gentile culture. Jews have played a leading role in producing and promoting the deconstruction of European painting, sculpture, music, and literature, as well as religion, social structures, and sexual mores.

Third, Jews have played a leading role in producing and promoting a shallow, synthetic mass popular culture—films, popular music, comics, and the like—which has been weaponized with propaganda promoting rootless cosmopolitanism and nihilism.

Jewish cultural appropriation, deconstruction, and weaponization are all deeply inauthentic and manipulative relationships to culture. But, then again, it is not *their* culture.

For Heidegger, we do not so much "have" a culture as culture "has" us. This is the meaning of Heidegger's concept of "*Ereignis*." We are appropriated or enthralled by culture. An authentic relationship to culture is a form of identification and belonging—in essence, rootedness—that does not allow us to objectify, manipulate, construct, or deconstruct it. A synthetic, weaponized culture is no culture at all. It is simply propaganda, a specific form of machinational history making. But Heidegger's remark can also be read as caution against National Socialist cultural politics falling into the same machinational and nihilistic Jewish pattern.

9.

. . . maybe in this "struggle" [*Kampf*] — which struggles over goallessness itself and which hence can be only the caricature of "struggle" — the greater groundlessness will "triumph" [*siegt*], which is bound to nothing and makes everything serviceable to itself (Jewry). (1938–1939; *GA* 95: 96–97)

In this passage, Heidegger puts in "scare quotes" two words with strong National Socialist connotations: *Kampf* (struggle, as in *Mein Kampf*) and *Sieg* (victory, as in "Sieg Heil.") The *Kampf* that Heidegger mentions here is the political, economic, cultural, and ideological battle between Germany and her opponents — primarily the British Empire and international Jewry — that eventually led to the outbreak of World War II. Heidegger places this "struggle" in quotation marks to indicate that he thinks that it is only a superficial "caricature of 'struggle.'"

Heidegger states that the present "struggle" is a caricature of real struggle because it is merely "over goallessness itself," i.e., nihilism without bounds. For Heidegger, the true struggle is between modernity and the new beginning for European man that he hoped National Socialism heralded. The fake struggles of his time, however, all take place on the plane of modernity. They are over alternatives *within* modernity, not alternatives *to* modernity. For Heidegger, the true struggle is *against* nihilism, not *between* different versions of it.

If this is the case, however, then Heidegger raises a chilling question: if the fake "struggle" of our time is between different forms of nihilism, wouldn't the most nihilistic party have a systematic advantage? Other things being equal, wouldn't the purer nihilists "triumph"? (Heidegger also puts "triumph" in scare quotes to indicate that victory on the plane of nihilism is just as superficial as the struggle for it.)

Heidegger calls the most nihilistic party the "greater groundlessness," meaning the least rooted and thus the most lacking in meaning and measure. The greater groundlessness is "bound to nothing," meaning that it has no limits on its possible actions, which means that it can "make everything serviceable to itself." The more grounded a nation, the more it is bound to a specific identity, and the fewer things it can make serviceable to itself.

Pure nihilists have no scruples, so they are willing to do anything to win. Impure nihilists are hampered by their residual scruples. Therefore, other things being equal, the purer nihilists will win. Heidegger indicates parenthetically that Jewry is the most nihilistic party in the current "struggle," thus the Germans are at a disadvantage.

The third and final passage is very clearly from a notebook. Heidegger's remarks are unusually cryptic, his thoughts jump from topic to topic without making the connections clear, and he entertains ideas that are not entirely consistent with his published views.

10.

The anti-Christian [*der Anti-christ*], like every "anti," must stem from the same essential ground as that against which it is "anti" — that is, the same essential ground as "the Christian" [*"der Christ"*]. The Christian stems from Jewry [*Judenschaft*]. In the timeframe of the Christian West, that is, of metaphysics, Judaism is the principle of destruction. What is destructive in the reversal of the completion of metaphysics — i.e., of Hegel's metaphysics by Marx. Spirit and culture become the superstructure of "life" — i.e., of economics, i.e., of organization — i.e., of the biological — i.e., of the "people."

When what is "Jewish" in the metaphysical sense combats what is Jewish, the high point of self-annihilation in history has been attained — supposing that the "Jewish" has everywhere completely seized mastery, so that even the fight against "the Jewish," and it above all, becomes subject to it.

On this basis one must assess what it means, for thinking that enters the concealed, inceptive essence of the history of the Occident, to meditate on the first inception among the Greeks, which remained outside Judaism and thus outside Christianity. (*circa.* 1942–1945; *GA* 97: 20)

Here Heidegger at least seems to ponder the possibility that *all* forms of opposition are futile, if indeed *all* opposition "must stem from the same essential ground as that against which it is 'anti.'" But perhaps Heidegger is overstating his case here. For is it really true that all opposition to Christianity somehow secretly affirms Christianity? Or is this true of only certain forms of opposition, such as secular liberal critiques which affirm and intensify Christian values?

Heidegger's thought process then jumps to the topic of Jewry.

Christianity is a product of Jewry, but it is unclear what connection this has to the previous point about anti-Christianity. Is Christian opposition to Jewry futile because Christianity stems from Jewry? Perhaps, but Heidegger's initial point is about anti-Christianity, not anti-Semitism.

Heidegger then jumps to a particularly pregnant statement: "In the timeframe of the Christian West, that is, of metaphysics, Judaism is the principle of destruction."

First, what does Heidegger mean by equating metaphysics and the timeframe of the Christian West? This is only a rough equation, since Western metaphysics emerged in ancient Greece, centuries before the emergence of Christianity, but Christianity and Greek metaphysics became fused in late antiquity.

Second, in what sense is Judaism the principle of destruction within the age of metaphysics and the Christian West? It would make more sense and be more consistent with Heidegger's other statements if he spoke of *Jewry* as a people rather than *Judaism* as a religion. Judaism is present in Christianity at the beginning, but the principle of destruction manifests itself near the end of Christianity and metaphysics, i.e., in the emergence of modernity, i.e., the age of rootlessness and unbounded technological nihilism, the metaphysically "Jewish" age in which Jewry rises to power and drives modernity to its completion.

Heidegger's next remark seems to be an illustration of this principle: Marx's inversion of Hegel's metaphysics, transforming the realm of spirit and culture into a superstructure upon an economic basis. But Heidegger then equates Marxist materialism with other philosophies that treat spirit and culture as manifestations of more basic material forces.

The first material force is "life," which Heidegger himself puts in quotes. This is an allusion to Nietzsche and the tradition of "life philosophy" (*Lebensphilosophie*) that took its bearings from Nietzsche. Then Heidegger cites two more materialist principles: the "biological" and the "people" (*Volk*), the latter term in quotes as well. This is an obvious reference to National Socialism.

Thus Heidegger is equating Marxism, Nietzscheanism, and National Socialism insofar as they are all forms of cultural materialism. Beyond that, Heidegger is equating materialism — and thus Nietzscheanism and National Socialism — with Judaism, the "principle of destruction" within the "timeframe of the Christian West."

In the next paragraph, Heidegger paints National Socialist anti-Semitism as a combat between "what is 'Jewish' in the metaphysical sense," i.e., National Socialism, and "what is Jewish" in the factual sense, namely world Jewry itself.

By putting "Jewish" in scare quotes, Heidegger distances himself from the usage of the word. He is using the word as National Socialists use it. But he is saying that they don't really know what they are talking about. What National Socialists call "Jewish" is simply modernity: rootlessness, globalization, and technological machination. But Heidegger's point is that National Socialism itself is "Jewish" in that sense of the word. The National Socialists thought they were fighting for rootedness and nationalism, but they unwittingly adopted the very ideas they rejected.

Thus National Socialist anti-Semitism and the war in general are "the high point of self-annihilation in history." It is "self-annihilation" because the opposed forces are the *same* insofar as they are both modernist, that is to say "Jewish," one in the metaphysical sense, the other in the factual sense.

To be clear, Heidegger is not saying that Jews in the factual sense are annihilating themselves, but that National Socialists and Jews are metaphysically the same (modern), so that in annihilating Jews, National Socialists are annihilating themselves. At first, Heidegger hoped that National Socialism would annihilate modernity. Later, he came to see World War II as modernity's annihilation of itself. The "self" that is engaged in annihilation here is not Jewry but modernity. Modernity encompasses Jewry but is not identical to it, since it encompasses National Socialism as well.[19]

If in modernity, *everything* is what National Socialists call "Jewish" — rootless and nihilistic — then all resistance to what is Jewish (in a metaphysical or a factual sense) will be "Jewish" as well. Which means that resistance is futile. But again, Heidegger is overstating his case, for here he is leaving out the possibility of a genuine alternative to modernity, and we know that he believed that such an alternative — a new beginning — was possible.

This possibility is hinted at in the final paragraph. The argument of the previous paragraph takes place entirely on the plane of modern nihilism, and on that plane, it is futile to resist one form of nihilism with another. In the final paragraph, however, Heidegger's discourse shifts to another plane. This shift is signaled by his reference to the "thinking that enters the

---

[19] Donatella Di Cesare erroneously interprets Heidegger's "self-annihilation" to refer exclusively to Jews in *Heidegger and the Jews: The Black Notebooks*, trans. Murtha Baca (Cambridge, UK: Polity Press, 2018), 201–202.

Robert Bernasconi makes the same mistake in "Another Eisenmenger? On the Alleged Originality of Heidegger's Antisemitism" in *Heidegger's Black Notebooks: Responses to Anti-Semitism*, ed. Andrew J. Mitchell and Peter Trawny (New York: Columbia University Press, 2017), 177–79.

concealed, inceptive essence of the history of the Occident," the realm from which metaphysics, modernity, and a new beginning might emerge.

How can such thinking contribute to a new beginning? Heidegger's only suggestion here is to "meditate on the first inception among the Greeks, which remained outside Judaism and thus outside Christianity." We can free ourselves from the Judeo-Christian cultural legacy by reconnecting with the other origin of Western civilization, namely pagan Greece. But this is not the whole story for Heidegger, because the ancient Greeks are also the source of the metaphysical tradition that gives rise to modern nihilism. Thus, we must attune ourselves specifically to the pre-Socratic, pre-metaphysical Greeks like Heraclitus.

Heidegger's reflections on the apparent futility of fighting against modern nihilism within the framework of modern nihilism, against Jewry within the framework of "metaphysical" Jewishness—as well as his suggestion that a genuine form of resistance is possible by drawing upon hidden resources outside the frameworks of metaphysics and the Christian West—raise two questions.

First, although Heidegger eventually came to see National Socialism as a form of modern nihilism rather than an alternative to it, does this mean that he believed that National Socialism and World War II were entirely illegitimate and futile exercises, compared to the other options available on the political plane? Heidegger correctly believed that World War II was set in motion by the organized Jewish community, which created a coalition of Soviet Communists and Anglo-Saxon capitalists. From the start, the war was a clash between technological titans, and although spiritual and ideological factors played a role, its outcome ultimately depended on the technical-instrumental capacity to muster and deploy human and natural resources in the most destructive way possible. Clearly, such a war could only advance rather than overthrow the modern world.

But did Heidegger believe that Germany could have fought any other way? Did Heidegger think that the Germans should not have fought at all? Did Heidegger think that Germany should have produced fewer bombs and more editions of Heraclitus and Hölderlin? Clearly not. From a Heideggerian point of view, National Socialism was a disappointment only because it did not amount to the radical new beginning Heidegger had hoped for. But given that the battle ultimately took place on the technological plane, the Germans clearly had to take a gun to a gunfight.

In the reflections on the war from around September 1941, from which passage no. 2 is taken, Heidegger seems to accept that there is at least a kind of conditional or provisional legitimacy of viewing the war in realistic terms, on the plane of clashing versions of nihilism.[20] And Heidegger is clearly on Germany's side. It might be futile to fight against bad metaphysics with guns, but one can still win a war with them. And clearly, if Germany had developed the atomic bomb before the Allies, and used it, she could have won.

World War II is over. The interwar fascist movements—which I call the Old Right—were defeated. But the New Right is continuing the battle on the metapolitical plane: creating and propagating new ways of seeing the world and dwelling in it. We are still fighting for nationalism against globalization, for rootedness against cosmopolitanism, for identity against homogeneity, individualism, consumerism, and inauthenticity. We are fighting for a world in which every people has a homeland, Jews included, but in which the deracinating, leveling, and homogenizing forces of cosmopolitan ideologies, global capitalism, transnational elites, and international Jewry have no power.

But this brings us to a second question: Given Heidegger's historical anti-humanism, can an individual or a movement do anything at all to produce historical change? Heidegger holds that movements to make and remake history are premised on a false understanding of how history works. Man cannot understand or control history. Thus we cannot engineer a new historical age. As noted, that does not stop people from trying. So isn't it a danger that people who take Heidegger to heart will simply stop trying to fight, surrendering the world to be trashed by nihilists who have no such scruples?

But Heidegger's historical anti-humanism does not lead to passivity and quietism.

First, for Heidegger, humanism is a false theory of man's relationship to history. But historical change and human agency are real. Heidegger wishes to discard the false theory and replace it with a better one. He does not wish to abandon human agency and historical change as such, except insofar as they are influenced by a false self-understanding. Human agency may not be what the humanists say it is, but it still exists, thus it is still possible to fight for a better world.

Second, although Heidegger does believe that man cannot understand and control historical change, he also holds that the relationship of man and historical-cultural meaning is one of mutual dependence: man cannot exist without meaning, and meaning cannot exist without man. Individually and collectively, humanity might be unable to control history, but by

---

[20] See Polt's translation, 8–9.

the same token, we do *sustain* cultural and historical meaning. Thus, to the extent that we can stop sustaining the present dispensation, we have some power in the relationship.[21]

Third, there is a sense in which Heidegger's anti-humanism is empowering to dissidents. On the humanist account, a dissenting idea is just the beginning of historical change. One must then create a movement and struggle for power just to get into the position to remake society according to one's own blueprint. In this fallen world, that is a daunting and depressing prospect indeed.

On the Heideggerian account, however, your dissenting idea is not just a quirk of an isolated brain but a sign that cultural change is already underway. The humanist thinks that he is a solitary genius who creates ideas separate from humanity and history and wants to impose his designs upon them. The Heideggerian knows that he is always already immersed in collective historical meaning. So if he is thinking dissenting thoughts, others probably are as well, and more will follow, for they are all simply responding to changes in the *Zeitgeist*. For Heidegger, philosophers and poets are not the hidden legislators of mankind, but simply those most sensitive to coming changes. This is why Heidegger occasionally slips into the prophetic voice.

But if the change we desire is already on the way, does this mean that we can simply sit back and let history do our job for us? No, because some of us are not just called to dissent, we are called to fight. But we go forth into battle with the assurance that the change we fight for is already in some sense real, and it is coming to meet us.

Greg Johnson has a Ph.D. in philosophy and is editor of Counter-Currents Publishing.

---

[21] For more on this matter, see my "Making Sense of Heidegger," *Counter-Currents*, December 12, 2014.

https://www.counter-currents.com/2014/12/making-sense-of-heidegger/

BLACK ANTI-SEMITISM

ANDREW JOYCE

[Jews] infiltrate the Negro neighborhood with stores, and they exploit the Negro more than any other White group—housing, food, clothing—controlling the three basic things Negroes need. They claim to be friendly with Negroes but, when pushed to the wall, they are more injurious, more ruthless, than other Whites.
Jeremiah X, 1965.[1]

Speaking to the Black historian Horace Mann Bond in 1965, Jeremiah X, then leader of the Atlanta Mosque of the Nation of Islam, argued that "the Jews are the Negro's worst enemy among whites." The reason Jews were particularly dangerous, explained Jeremiah, was the fact they "make it a practice to study Negroes; thus they are able to get next to him better than the other whites. He uses the knowledge thus obtained to get close to the Negro, thereby being in a position to stab him with a knife." This metaphorical knife was both economic and socio-cultural. As well as acting as slumlord, pawnbroker, and merchant, the Jew of the Black world was also a manipulative political actor: "Through their control of the press and of other mass media they are able to make the public feel sorry for Jews. It is so bad today that anybody who speaks out against Jews is immediately clobbered as 'anti-Semitic.' They have made the Negroes to believe their sufferings have been greater than those of the Negro in America."

This is an interesting perspective, to say the least, and for as long as I've been interested in anti-Semitism, I've been intrigued by the expression of hostility towards Jews among non-Whites. My reasons should be obvious. As I've written previously, concerning anti-Semitism in South Korea,

---

[1] Horace Mann Bond "Negro Attitudes Towards Jews," *Jewish Social Studies*, 27, no. 1, Papers and Proceedings of a Conference on Negro-Jewish Relations in the United States (January, 1965), 3–9.

one of the most fundamental positions for White advocates concerned with Jewish influence must be the conviction that antagonism against Jews lies in Jewish behavior rather than solely the cultural pathology or psychological tendencies of non-Jews. A major testing ground for this position is the necessity for anti-Jewish attitudes to be present among geographically, racially, and culturally diverse peoples, and for the reasons behind this antagonism to be fairly uniform.[2]

Black anti-Semitism in the United States is especially interesting in its own right for historical and contemporary cultural, economic, social, and political reasons. From at least the time of the Civil War, Jews, Blacks, and Whites have existed in a fateful racial triad, and Black anti-Semitism has much to tell us about all three groups, the relations between them, and the very nature of anti-Semitism itself. Black anti-Semitism has also maintained a constant, though often low-key, quality, with sporadic violent outbreaks since at least the first decade of the twentieth century, the most recent being the spate of assaults in December, 2019.[3] Of equal importance to the reasons behind this hostility is the Jewish response, and how that response molds Jewish understandings of anti-Semitism and determines the character of Jewish apologetics for their own antagonistic behaviors. The Jewish response to Black anti-Semitism will be the subject of Part II of this article, while Part I is primarily intended to provide an overview of some of the main aspects of Black anti-Semitism and its meaning and value to White advocacy. As such, it should be seen as complimenting and extending Kevin MacDonald's essay "Jews, Blacks, and Race," included in the 2007 volume *Cultural Insurrections*.[4]

---

[2] Andrew Joyce, "Paul Singer and the Universality of 'Anti-Semitism,'" *The Occidental Observer* (August 1, 2015).
https://www.theoccidentalobserver.net/2015/08/01/paul-singer-and-universality-of-anti-semitism/

[3] Jay Michselson, "What's Behind the New Wave of Anti-Semitic Hate?," *The Daily Beast* (December 30, 2019).
https://www.thedailybeast.com/whats-behind-the-new-wave-in-anti-semitic-hate

[4] Kevin MacDonald, "Jews, Blacks, and Race," in Samuel Francis (ed.), *Race and the American Prospect: Essays on the Racial Realities of Our Nation and Our Time* (Atlanta: The Occidental Press, 2006), 330–356; reprinted in Kevin MacDonald, *Cultural Insurrections* (Atlanta: The Occidental Press, 2007), 196–222.

PART I: FEATURES OF BLACK ANTI-SEMITISM

In *Separation and Its Discontents*, Kevin MacDonald identifies the key historical themes of anti-Semitism as including an understanding that, speaking in general terms, Jews

- represent a separate and clannish foreign group with their own set of interests;
- are highly adept at resource competition and have a tendency towards economic domination;
- tend to engage as cultural actors in order to shape non-Jewish culture to suit Jewish interests;
- form a cohesive political entity that seeks politically dominant roles in non-Jewish societies;
- possess negative personality traits, including the pursuance of a system of dual ethics in which non-Jews can be treated badly and exploited;
- are disloyal to the host nation in all fundamental and meaningful ways

Among the factors mitigating anti-Semitism, one of the most crucial contemporary elements has been the Jewish promotion of multi-ethnic, pluralist societies. As MacDonald explains, "a multicultural society in which Jew are simply one of many tolerated groups is likely to meet Jewish interests, because there is a diffusion of power among a variety of groups and it becomes impossible to develop homogeneous gentile in-groups arrayed against Jews as a highly conspicuous group."[5] Of particular interest, then, is the extent to which the key themes of anti-Semitism manifest among Blacks, how they manifest, and how the Black position of being a celebrated component feature of pluralism (rather than, as in the case of Whites, being the majority population subjected to pluralism) impacts the mitigation of anti-Semitism.

Common sense would suggest that each ethnic group will inflect the themes of anti-Semitism according the context and precise nature of their own interaction with Jews. In South Korea, organized anti-Jewish hostility was built around the understanding that Jewish financiers, mainly American, with a history of highly exploitative behaviors, were attempting to gain strongholds in South Korean companies like Samsung.[6] As

---

[5] Kevin MacDonald, *Separation and Its Discontents: Toward and Evolutionary Theory of anti-Semitism* (FirstBooks, 2004; originally published: Westport, CT: Praeger, 1998), 87.

[6] Joyce, "Paul Singer and the Universality of 'Anti-Semitism.'"

such, the primary theme of anti-Semitism in South Korea has been the understanding that Jews are dangerously adept at resource competition, are financially ruthless and exploitative, are highly ethnocentric, and are powerful in the media and in politics at the highest levels. During the early stages of an attempted expansion of influence by the almost entirely Jewish vulture fund Elliot Associates, *Media Pen* columnist Kim Ji-ho claimed "Jewish money has long been known to be ruthless and merciless." This was soon followed by the former South Korean ambassador to Morocco, Park Jae-seon, expressing his concern about the influence of Jews in finance when he said, "The scary thing about Jews is they are grabbing the currency markets and financial investment companies. Their network is tight-knit beyond one's imagination." A day later, cable news channel YTN aired similar comments by local journalist Park Seong-ho, airing the opinion that "it is a fact that Jews use financial networks and have influence wherever they are born."

Among Blacks, the same themes have been inflected in less elevated terms, arising first from more modest economic conflicts and, as such, having something more in common with the complaints of the early modern European peasantries. Horace Mann Bond, in his own 1965 reflections in his "Negro Attitudes Toward Jews," comments on the fact Jews historically appeared in the African-American environment overwhelmingly as pawnbrokers, as monopolists of the liquor trade ("The Jews have a stranglehold on the liquor stores in this town"), as the primary sellers on credit of clothing and other essential items, and, perhaps most crucial of all, as the slumlord and property dealer, e.g., "Some Jews have bought up that urban re-development land and are putting up shoddy apartments they call "Nigger housing" on it.[7] In 2016, local news website *Patch* published a list of the 100 worst slumlords in Harlem,[8] with the top ten including seven Jews (Mark Silber, Adam Stryker, Joel Goldstein, Marc Chemtob, Moshe Deutsch, Solomon Gottlieb, Jason Green), a representation that has remained roughly constant every year, with Jews persistently claiming top ranking for building violations, rodent infestations, lack of maintenance, exploitative rent, mold, and other forms of building decay injurious to health.

---

[7] Bond "Negro Attitudes Towards Jews," 5.

[8] Brenden Krisel, "Who's the Worst Landlord in Harlem? See Who Made the Cut," *Patch* (October 14, 2016).
https://patch.com/new-york/harlem/whos-worst-landlord-harlem-see-who-made-cut

Indeed, it is the sheer dominance and proximity of the Jews as primary exploiters of Blacks that has often caused a quite radical break in the Black imagination between perceiving wholesale "White oppression," and the more nuanced understanding that Jews are a distinctive class unto themselves. Moreover, the reality of day-to-day interethnic exploitation leaves little room for abstract apologetic theories of anti-Semitism, since the problem is never that Jews arouse hostility merely on account of their religion or identity, but rather that Jews arouse hostility because of their behavior within certain ecological contexts. As Bond explains,

> It is my considered view that Negro attitudes and actions towards Jews that are frequently interpreted as "antisemitic" actually lack the sinister thought-content they are sometimes advertised as holding. The occasional riots against small businessmen and landlords in Harlem—persons who may happen to be Jews—do not, in my opinion, actually possess the "classic" emotional load of aggression against a Jewish "race" or "religion," that has been considered the essence of antisemitism.[9]

I think Bond, in this instance, waters down the specificity of anti-Jewish hostility that eventually develops, because it's more or less inevitable in the context of social identity theory that if someone is negatively confronted on enough occasions with "persons who may happen to be Jews," then they will eventually be forced to make an evaluation of Jews as a group. Bond, however, is of course accurate in pointing out that it's perfectly possible for anti-Jewish actions to occur without the "sinister thought-content" often theorized and expounded upon in Jewish apologetics. Reading between the lines, Bond clearly interprets small-scale violence against these particular Jews as ad hoc reactions to local financial exploitation, an interpretive framework that by contrast has only been employed at the smallest of levels, and with the most minimum impact, when discussing anti-Jewish riots in the European past. Of further value is Bond's doubting of the putative essence of anti-Semitism, "the classic emotional load of aggression" on the basis of race or religion, which again has only served to distance understandings of anti-Semitism from the realities of antagonistic Jewish group behaviors.

A lot of what has been discussed above is clearly resource-oriented, and economic competition between Blacks and Jews, devastatingly one-

---

[9] Bond "Negro Attitudes Towards Jews," 7.

sided to be sure, goes right back to the arrival of the African in the Americas. Writing in a 1977 edition of the *Negro History Bulletin*, Oscar R. Williams comments that, unlike, the Quakers, the Jews never adopted a position on slavery as a group in the period prior to the Civil War. Moreover,

> the presence of the Southern Jews complimented the system of slavery; their mercantilist interest made slavery a more effective labor system. While most Jews were not to be found on plantations, their activities made the plantation a self-sufficient unit. What was not produced on the plantation was delivered by Jewish merchants. The Southern Jew has as much, if not more, to gain from the system of maintaining slavery as any other white segment within the South. During the Civil War Jews defended the system which insured them acceptance and success in the South. Neither the Civil War nor Reconstruction changed the Southern Jews' perception of Blacks as an animal to be used and exploited.[10]

While some initial divergence of opinion on race could be found between Northern and Southern Jews, the advent of the New South, and then the mass migration of Jews to the United States from Eastern Europe in 1880s, provoked a coalescence of Jewish behaviors in relation to Blacks.[11]

> Often in the New South, success of Jewish merchants depended on winning Black trade. Jewish merchants appeared more courteous and obviously spent more time with Black customers than fellow white merchants. Blacks were often victims of sales pressure when Jews refused to accept no-sale for an answer. No became the signal for the ritual to begin. Merchants would insist that the potential buyer try-on the item. After this came what Blacks call "Jewing Down," in which naive Blacks were led to believe that Jewish merchant had allowed himself to be beaten on the price.[12]

The post-Civil War movement of Blacks to the Northern cities coincided with the mass migration of East European Jews into the same urban centers. Boasting centuries of experience in the economic exploitation of

---

[10] Oscar P. Williams, "Historical Impressions of Black-Jewish Relations Prior to World War II". *Negro History Bulletin* 40, no. 4 (1977): 728-731, 728.

[11] *Ibid.*

[12] *Ibid.*

the lowest classes, Jews quickly set about the establishment of pawn shops, credit sales, and other methods of lending small-to-medium amounts of cash at interest.

Such was the scale of Jewish exploitation of urban Blacks in some areas that W.E.B. Du Bois was moved in 1903 to declare "The Jew is heir to the slavebaron."[13] And yet, growing alongside this exploitation was something hinted at by Williams. The Jews did in fact appear more courteous than Whites, even if their behavior didn't quite match the outward courtesy. And Jews did obviously spend more time with Black customers than did White merchants. The Black could be "Jewed Down" into believing he'd won himself a bargain, and he could also be "Jewed Down" into the belief that he had a friend and a helper in the form of the Jew, even if this illusion could last only for a short period, and all while the interest clock kept on ticking. Writing in *Commentary* in 1945, Kenneth B. Clark recounted how Blacks in Baltimore were pointing out that

> Jewish merchants own and control the major downtown department stores. ... Some Negro domestics assert that Jewish housewives who employ them are unreasonable and brazenly exploitative. A Negro actor states in bitter terms that he is being flagrantly underpaid by a Jewish producer. A Negro entertainer is antagonistic to his Jewish agent who he is convinced is exploiting him. ... Antagonism toward the "Jewish landlord" is so common as to have become almost an integral aspect of the folk culture of the northern urban Negro.[14]

It is indeed a curious feature of American history that the growth of the Black-Jewish civil rights alliance should have coincided with the intensification of Jewish exploitation of Blacks. During the 1920s, the same decade that the mostly Jewish-run NAACP began a serious escalation in agitation for "civil rights," Jews were invading Black areas in Northern cities, using their growing political influence to engage in the exploitation of Blacks and the suppression of their local businesses. In *Jews and Booze: Becoming American in the Age of Prohibition*, Marni Davis comments on the Harlem newspaper *The Age* which complained throughout the early 1920s about Jews who

---

[13] Maurianne Adams (ed.), *Strangers and Neighbors: Relations Between Blacks and Jews in the United States* (Amherst: University of Massachusetts Press, 1999), 18.

[14] Kenneth B. Clark, "Candor about Jewish-Negro Relations," *Commentary*, 1 (December 1, 1945), 8.

had bought the police, fouled Harlem with their liquor, and were now poisoning the locals (sometimes literally) and siphoning away the neighborhood's hard-earned capital. … *The Age* noted that many of the stores in question had the name "Hyman" attached to them. They all turned out to be owned by Hyman Kassel [other liquor traders in Harlem included Izzy Einstein, Connie Immerman, and Dutch Schultz], a well-known bootlegger and numbers runner. … "Hebrew Operators Control Lenox Avenue Places," blared one headline. … The accusations levelled by *The Age* resembled nativist claims that Jews were economic parasites and moral defilers.[15]

Davis comments that Jews "regarded the anti-alcohol movement as politically wrong-headed — even repulsive — and certainly as inimical to the civil liberties guaranteed by the Constitution," but such explanations for Jewish opposition to the temperance movement (conservative, Christian, family-oriented) are glaring in their avoidance of the fact Jews possessed centuries of experience in exploiting the sale of liquor to the lowest classes in Eastern Europe in order to obtain and maintain political, social, and economic advancement and control.[16] In other words, the argument that Jews pursed the often harmful sale of liquor purely out of abstract concern for "rights" and freedoms is a rather convenient way of side-stepping obvious, and often criminal, self-interest.

During the 1930s and 1940s, Jewish dominance of the trade in furniture, household items, and other essentials in the Black sections of Northern cities led to the development of the idea among Blacks in several cities that Jews "only posed as friends." These decades witnessed "rent strikes, business boycotts, and other forms of economic pressure," as well as riots that were "tinged with anti-Semitic feeling," all of which very closely resembled actions in Eastern Europe around 50 years earlier that had been characterized in contemporary propaganda as irrational and barbaric pogroms.[17] In fact, the causes of both sets of actions are almost entirely identical, with Steven Gold remarking in his fascinating 2010 *The Store in the Hood: A Century of Ethnic Business and Conflict* that between the 1930s

---

[15] Marni Davis, *Jews and Booze: Becoming American in the Age of Prohibition* (New York: NYU Press, 2012), 163.

[16] See Glenn Dynner, *Yankel's Tavern: Jews, Liquor, and Life in the Kingdom of Poland* (Princeton, NJ: Princeton University Press, 2014).

[17] C. Rottenberg, *Black Harlem and the Jewish Lower East Side: Narratives Out of Time* (New York: State University of New York Press, 2013), 128.

and 1960s Jews "owned many of the largest businesses in ghettos, including department stores, hardware stores, and furniture stores."[18] Even as Jews moved into the suburbs, unlike other ethnic groups, they retained as much economic influence in Black areas as possible, resulting in their becoming "out-group entrepreneurs and absentee landlords."[19] John Bracey comments:

> No other group paid [the Black] the slightest attention: not the Germans, nor the Irish, nor the Poles, nor the Italians, not the Hungarians, nor the Slovaks; only the Jew established a line of communication, albeit a line of communication in trade and credit merchandising. True, the Jew had an advantage. To him the American Negro was no different from the Gentile peasants among whom he lived and with whom he dealt in the towns and villages of Russia, Galicia, Hungary, and Poland.[20]

Gold notes that everywhere in these areas Jews and Blacks existed within a framework of "power and control," and "the context within which African-American women were hired and then supervised in Jewish homes was especially humiliating. At least in New York, this practice came to be known as the "Bronx Slave Market." After public complaints, the La Guardia administration (1934–1945) created employment offices to provide Black domestic workers with an additional measure of security and dignity."[21]

The period 1945–1960s is often presented in mainstream historiography and social science as involving a Black-Jewish alliance in the pursuit of civil rights for African-Americans. Kevin MacDonald's theory that this alliance was essentially an almost-entirely Jewish-operated venture in pursuit of Jewish goals and interests (the breaking up, via legislation and cultural change, of notions of America as a White country) has been maligned as itself anti-Semitic, despite the fact such interpretations are present even among Jewish scholars in the academic mainstream. Seymour Weisman, for example, writing in a 1980 edition of the Routledge journal *Patterns of Prejudice*, comments that "there was an obvious Jewish

---

[18] Steven J. Gold, *The Store in the Hood: A Century of Ethnic Business and Conflict* (New York: Rowman & Littlefield, 2010), 73.

[19] *Ibid.*, 74.

[20] J. Bracey (ed), *Strangers and Neighbors: Relations Between Blacks and Jews in the United States* (Amherst: University of Massachusetts Press, 1999), 571.

[21] *Ibid.*

self-interest to promote legislation and initiate judicial actions" that would broaden the ethnic nature of the United States.[22]

The issue of Jewish self-interest is important because of the obvious implication of rhetorical insincerity. Much like apologetic narratives arguing that Jews traded in liquor, often via monopoly, because they believed in individual rights and freedoms, there are certainly grounds for doubting Jewish claims that they engage in "social justice" work out of sincere belief in the equality of Man. A particularly interesting case in this regard is related by Jeffrey Gurock in his *The Jews of Harlem: The Rise, Decline, and Revival of a Jewish Community*, where he recounts the great disillusionment of Blacks in late 1950s in the Bronx on discovering that despite copious public Jewish rhetoric on racial equality, when a predominantly Jewish school in a predominantly Jewish neighborhood (and with a Jewish principal) "accepted five classes of Negroes" from a nearby school, they "isolated them on a separate floor."[23]

Seymour Weisman claimed in 1981 that it was something of a great mystery that "the breakdown of Black-Jewish relations" should have occurred "at that precise moment in history when the civil rights legislative battle had been won."[24] In truth, the breakdown only takes on a mysterious aspect if one firstly believes the Black-Jewish alliance to have been sincere in the first place, and, secondly, that if one believes that Jews were sincere in the putative concern for the welfare and well-being of Blacks as a matter of "social justice" rather than as a tool to dismantling White America. Historical data would instead suggest that Jews were prominent exploiters of Blacks who rather expertly and skillfully created an image of themselves as friends and allies of Blacks. It goes without saying that once Jewish goals in pursuing such a masquerade had been accomplished, the Jewish effort in sustaining the positive but illusory aspects of such a relationship would dramatically decline. In the absence of rhetorical smoke and mirrors, all that remained was the constant of mundane economic, social, and political exploitation in the Black heartlands. This is what has simmered since the 1960s, and this is what bubbled to the surface once again in November 2019.

---

[22] Seymour S. Weisman (1980) "Black-Jewish relations in the USA — I: One year after the Andrew Young affair," *Patterns of Prejudice* 14, no. 4 (1980): 18–28.

[23] Jeffrty Gurock, *The Jews of Harlem: The Rise, Decline, and Revival of a Jewish Community* (New York: New York University Press, 2016), 213.

[24] Seymour S. Weisman, "Black-Jewish relations in the USA — II," *Patterns of Prejudice* 15, no. 1 (1981): 45–52.

A fascinating feature of coverage of the Winter 2019–2020 attacks on Jews by Blacks in New York has been the total absence of media enquiry into why the assaults took place. Like so much historiography on European anti-Semitism, there is simply no room for a serious attempt at explanation. As in Kiev, or Odessa, or the Rhine Valley, or Lincoln, or Aragon, or Galicia, the assaults on Jews in Brooklyn apparently emerged from the ether, motivated by some miasmic combination of insanity and demonic aggression. NBC New York reported bluntly on a "spree of hate,"[25] but had nothing in the way of analysis of context other than a condemnation of "possible hate-based attacks"—one of the most remarkably opaque pieces of analytical nomenclature I've ever come across. Former New York State Assemblyman Dov Hikind has said "The attacks against Jews are out of control, and we must have a concrete strategy to address the rise of these attacks." But how he can develop a strategy to address something that apparently does not yet have an explanation is another question left unanswered.

PART II: JEWISH REACTIONS TO BLACK ANTI-SEMITISM

Jews often become convenient stand-ins as the purveyors of the structures of systemic racism that continue to plague Black America.

Tema Smith, explaining attacks by Blacks on Jews in December 2019.[26]

Being well-organized, Jewish communal associations took note when Jewish merchants were accused of inappropriate behavior. When African-American journalists or activists complained about the exploitative behavior of ghetto merchants, Jewish spokesmen often resisted accepting responsibility and instead labeled accusers as anti-Semites for referring to the merchants' religion. Contending that Jewish merchants treated Blacks no worse than other Whites did, they objected to being singled out.

Steven Gold on the Jewish response to growing Black anti-Semitism in 1940s Harlem.[27]

---

[25] Erica Byfield and Myles Miller, "Open Season on Jews: Outrage over Spike in in NYC Hate Attacks," *NBC News* (December 28, 2019).
https://www.nbcnewyork.com/news/local/crime-and-courts/open-season-on-jews-reports-of-anti-semitic-attacks-during-hanukkah-cause-for-concern/2250584/
[26] Tema Smith, "How to Talk about Black Anti-Semitism," *Forward* (January 9, 2020).
https://temasmith.com/portfolio/how-to-talk-about-Black-anti-semitism/
[27] Gold, *The Store in the Hood*, 75.

As remarked in "Part I," it's clear that visible and occasionally violent Black hostility towards Jews presents the latter with an objective problem in terms of their (publicly expressed) self-concept as a people and the received wisdom regarding the nature of anti-Semitism (now given quasi-legal standing in many countries via the International Holocaust Remembrance Alliance definition[28]). In general terms, Jews have tended to avoid any sense of responsibility for anti-Semitism by creating and promoting narratives in which they are passive victims of a phenomenon that is the result of fundamentally irrational bigotry. This is often accompanied by the insistence that anti-Semitism has its origins in what are seen as pathological elements in European Christianity and that anti-Semitism is little more than a set of ideas that act as a viral psychosis among Whites.

Since the early twentieth century, this understanding has been augmented with a variety of modifications, many derived from Marxism and psychoanalysis, but the essential argument that anti-Semitism is a White pathology has survived, and has been very widely disseminated in Western cultural, political, and educational spheres. In fact, it has been challenged in significant terms only by the rise of anti-Jewish hostility in the Middle East, but even in that instance it has been characterized by Jewish historians like Bernard Lewis as being influenced by Europeans.[29] Within the West, and omitting anti-Semitism among Muslim immigrants, the periodic spike in anti-Jewish hostility among American Blacks represents perhaps the only persistent Western challenge to the received wisdom that anti-Semitism is a White problem, rather than a problem that originates with Jewish behavior. Black anti-Semitism also problematizes notions that Jews have been selfless and valuable allies to Blacks and other minorities, something that has been a key aspect of Jewish propaganda campaigns for pluralism in Western nations. As such, Jewish rhetorical and legal responses to Black anti-Semitism are of interest to White advocates, and to all peoples concerned with Jewish/Zionist group influence and behavior.

---

[28] "Defining Anti-Semitism," U.S. State Department (n.d.; accessed June 18, 2020). https://www.state.gov/defining-anti-semitism/

[29] Bernard Lewis, "Global Anti-Semitism Has Spread Throughout the Muslim World Like a Cancer," *The Washington Post* (February 14, 2019).
https://www.washingtonpost.com/opinions/global-opinions/anti-semitism-has-spread-through-the-muslim-world-like-a-cancer/2019/02/14/1ba5b91a-30aa-11e9-8ad3-9a5b113ecd3c_story.html

VICTIMS OF WHITE SYSTEMS

One of the most prominent Jewish strategies when discussing Black anti-Semitism is the attempt to preserve both Jewish and Black senses of victimhood, and thus preserve the idea of an alliance against an allegedly oppressive White society. On the most basic level, this strategy involves denying any specificity to Black complaints against Jews and essentially involves an entrenchment of the idea that anti-Semitism is a White pathology. Black socio-economic grievances are radically downplayed or even ignored entirely in this framework, and the locus of all discussion tends to be on vague, putative historical contexts of Jewish victimhood (e.g. "This is another sorry chapter in the history of the Longest Hatred"), rather than on serious thinking about perpetrator motivation.

An excellent example in this regard is Tema Smith's *Forward* article "How to Talk about Black Anti-Semitism."[30] Smith attempts to preserve both Jewish and Black senses of victimhood by arguing that "Jews often become convenient stand-ins as the purveyors of the structures of systemic racism that continue to plague Black America." This is really a fascinating statement given that it comes in the aftermath of Black attacks on Jews involving everything from "fists and stones to machetes, automatic weapons, and explosive devices." Despite very clear dynamics of targeted hostility, the victimhood of both peoples is preserved and asserted since the putatively passive Jews are merely "convenient stand-ins," and Blacks are themselves "plagued" by "the structures of systemic racism." In other words, antagonistic Jewish behaviors are either non-existent or ultimately irrelevant, while Blacks can't be fully condemned for their attitudes and behavior because they've essentially been fooled by an exploitative racist system. Thus, in a context in which a disproportionately vast numbers of Hasidic Jews exploit their tenants and accumulate hundreds of building violations through sheer greed and disdain for those living in their properties, and in the process making life hell for many Blacks, the real villain of the story is somehow the White man—a figure, curiously enough, that is almost totally absent from all "Worst Landlord" lists.

In this reaction, therefore, Jews and their behaviors dissolve into the abstraction of imagined social systems—specifically "racist" systems that are part of a putative White power structure. Smith continues:

What is remarkable, though, is that a single factor underlies every attempt to diagnose a unique form of Black anti-Semitism: systemic

30 Smith, "How to Talk about Black Anti-Semitism."

racism. In analysis after analysis, antisemitism in the Black community is shown to be the symptom of the structures of racism in the United States — housing insecurity, lack of access to quality education, food deserts, access to political capital, discriminatory policing, and on and on. Ultimately, the conversation about Black anti-Semitism is not actually about Blacks and Jews.

This is a capable use of persuasive language, but what is truly remarkable is that Smith fails to identify the true "single factor" underlying attempts to diagnose Black anti-Semitism — the stunning avoidance of any significant confrontation with the worst aspects of Jewish behavior in Black districts. Whether or not housing insecurity, lack of access to quality education, food deserts, access to political capital, or discriminatory policing have anything to do with the specific issue of Black anti-Semitism is up for debate, but what is clearly contributing to Black anti-Semitism is the decades-old prevalence of Jews as the very worst of ghetto slumlords, pawn brokers, loan merchants, and political hypocrites. Smith doesn't provide a single reference or footnote to any of the examples of "analysis after analysis" allegedly proving a thesis that conveniently absolves Jews of provoking Black aggression because these analyses are almost non-existent outside the ridiculous offerings of the Jewish power structure's own self-defense bodies. In fact, when serious, unbiased scholarly studies are made of Black anti-Semitism they tend to overwhelmingly conclude, in the words of Ronald Tsukashima and Darrel Montero, that "economic mistreatment [by Jews] is strongly related to heightened antipathy toward Jews."[31]

One study that concedes economic mistreatment of Blacks by Jews, but insists that Whites and their "racist system" are still responsible for the situation, is the ADL-sponsored *Anti-Semitism in America* (1979) by Harold Quinley and Charles Glock. In the fourth chapter of this text, "Anti-Semitism Among Black Americans," the authors concede their findings "are consistent with a theory that Black anti-Semitism is economically based," and that having business contacts with Jews "was associated with

---

[31] Ronald Tadao Tsukashima, Darrel Montero, "The Contact Hypothesis: Social and Economic Contact and Generational Changes in the Study of Black Anti-Semitism," *Social Forces* 55, no. 1 (September 1976), 149–165.

Although more ambiguous in their representation of findings, see also, Gary T. Marx, *Protest and Prejudice: A Study of Belief in the Black Community* (New York: Harper and Row, 1967) and Harold Quinley and Charles Glock, *Antisemitism in America* (New York: Free Press, 1979).

a sharp rise in anti-Semitic responses."[32] In particular, it was found that Jewish credit practices were one of the "principle areas in which Blacks are exploited. They often end up paying exorbitant prices for inferior goods."[33] Remarkably, however, in summarizing their conclusions, the authors move away radically from the specificities of Black-Jewish interactions, instead abstracting into discussion of systems of racism. In essence, they replicate the process of Jews dissolving into Whiteness. For example, they assert that "it is largely as members of the oppressive white majority that Blacks seem to react to Jews."[34] This is followed by what amounts to absolution of both Blacks and Jews, and a condemnation of Whites:

> Prejudice should be deplored wherever it exists and for whatever reason. At the same time, prejudice toward the oppressor is not to be equated with prejudice toward the oppressed. The prejudice of Blacks is in part a response to circumstances which white-dominated culture has imposed on them. The opposite does not apply with respect to the prejudice of whites.[35]

The rhetorical pattern is thus replicated that negative Jewish behavior is either non-existent or irrelevant, that, in a sense, Black violence is excusable, and that the real enemy of both is White people and their culture.

THE JUDEO-BOLSHEVIK INFLECTION

Part of the "racist system" apologetic, but worthy of analysis in its own right, is the Jewish-Marxist treatment of Black anti-Semitism. A good example of this approach is Aaron Freedman's article, "To Defeat Antisemitism, We Must Defeat Capitalism," published in *Jacobin*.[36] It's long been my opinion that a significant element of historical Jewish support for Marxism is that Marxism is itself a kind of "escape into systems." Jews have for centuries been noted as particularly negative forces within capitalism, and it would appear that Jews have much to gain by advancing the idea that it is the system of capitalism, rather than Judaism and Jewish

---

[32] Quinley and Glock, *Antisemitism in America*, 57.

[33] *Ibid.*, 66.

[34] *Ibid.*, 72.

[35] *Ibid.*

[36] Aaron Freedman, "To Defeat Antisemitism, We Must Defeat Capitalism," *Jacobin* (January, 2020).
https://jacobinmag.com/2020/01/antisemitism-capitalism-new-york-attacks

approaches to capitalism, that is inherently bad. It is indeed a curio of history and contemporary economics that Jews have heavily accumulated wealth and often dominated, in those economic areas widely seen as exemplifying the worst of capitalism: usury/high interest loans, including the modern payday loan; sub-prime mortgages; tax farming; vulture funds; monopoly; fraud; Ponzi schemes; slumlordism; tax avoidance; internet gambling; and malicious bankruptcy. I've tackled the Marxist critique of anti-Semitism in great detail in relation to the ideas of Slavoj Žižek.[37] Žižek later referenced the "true anti-Semitism" of my essay, but—rather tellingly—offered no rebuttal, refusing even to answer the question he quotes.[38] But here I want to discuss it specifically with reference to the issue of Black anti-Semitism.

Aaron Freedman, who lives in Brooklyn and should therefore know better, is quite unabashed in asserting that "Antisemitism endures because capitalist oppression needs a scapegoat"—really no more than a rephrasing of Tema Smith's claim that Jews are merely "convenient stand-ins" for the real problem: the racist structure of White society. Freedman admits that there has been a sudden increase in Black attacks on Jews, but his first attempt at explanation can only be described as nothing less than remarkable: "A surge in white-nationalist activity since Donald Trump's election is surely the main part of the story."

Inserting "surely" into a sentence is a nice effort at persuasive writing, but the logical gap is so great in this instance that it resembles the rhetorical equivalent of putting a band-aid on the hull of a sinking ship. Freedman qualifies his astonishing claim only by adding "but Trump's victory alone does not explain the spate of incidents in New York, committed in many cases by Black individuals in both planned assaults and apparently random street encounters." The confusion unfortunately escalates from there, with Freedman commenting "The Right obviously does not have an answer." The problem here is that we obviously do have an answer for the causes of Black anti-Semitism, and like all great theses it can be summed up in a single, short sentence: "Jews have been behaving badly

---

[37] Andrew Joyce, "Slavoj Žižek's 'Pervert's Guide to Anti-Semitism,'" *The Occidental Observer* (November 11, 2019).
https://www.theoccidentalobserver.net/2019/11/20/slavoj-zizeks-perverts-guide-to-anti-semitism/
[38] Slavoj Žižek, "The Trouble Is Not with the Jews, but with My Accusers," *RT* (December 11, 2019).
https://www.rt.com/op-ed/475552-independent-jews-slavoj-zizek/

again." Freedman dodges any hint at such an explanation, moving into his own breakdown of why Blacks have been attacking Jews: Capitalism.

Like all Marxist interpretations of anti-Semitism, Freedman asserts that "Its roots in the United States, by way of Europe, come from Christian discrimination against "Christ killers," dating as far back as the 2nd century CE." This is, quite frankly, a nonsensical oversimplification, and the dating of the origins of anti-Semitism from medieval Christendom, rather than the ancient world, is a depressingly common feature of Jewish apologetics, a tactic that typically owes much of its development to the convenience of placing the blame for anti-Semitism on early Christianity.

Most significantly, it is based on the theories of Gavin Langmuir, a philosemitic scholar who by his own admission dated his discussion of the origins of anti-Semitism to the medieval period because, "I am respectably knowledgeable only about the history of the West since the fall of the Roman Empire and am most at home in the Middle Ages." Compounding Freedman's gross errors, the *Jacobin* journalist states with brazen duplicity that Jewish financial activities in the Middle Ages were "far less oppressive" than that of other peoples (again, see my commentary on the ideas of Slavoj Žižek for historical sources contradicting such assertions[39]), and that they were only quaintly engaged in "petty bourgeois profit-seeking." No mention of Jewish alliance with elites or their often-privileged status. No discussion of Jewish tax-farming. No inclusion of peasant revolts against the unusually oppressive nature of Jewish finance. Jews appear in Freedman's narrative only as "a religious other," picked on because they were "also very vulnerable." So vulnerable they typically had royal protection? So vulnerable that most of the oldest residential houses in England were built for Jews, their thick stone standing the test of centuries and countless reactions from the goyim?

If by now, like me, you're wondering what Freedman has to say specifically on the matter of Black anti-Semitism, then also, like me, you'll be frustrated with the fact he finishes the piece without mentioning anything at all about Black anti-Jewish hostility in Brooklyn. In a grand piece of diversionary nonsense, he merely recounts the standard Judeo-Bolshevik narrative of anti-Semitism, declaring Black anti-Semitism to be inconsequential to the greater story: "the specific threat of white-nationalist organizations remains the paramount one," and "in any society in which the few rule over the many, racist and antisemitic victim-blaming will thrive." The message is therefore more or less identical to that offered by

---

[39] Joyce, "Slavoj Žižek's 'Pervert's Guide to Anti-Semitism.'"

Tema Smith—when Blacks attack Jews it has nothing to do with either Blacks or Jews, and everything to do with Whites. The situation thus presents itself that Jewish slumlords abuse and exploit their Black tenants, Blacks react by assaulting Jews, and Whites are encouraged to chastise themselves for causing it all through their evil desire for private property.

PLEADING IGNORANCE

In Part I I noted that there has been a complete absence of media inquiry as to the causes of the assaults. Mirroring media neglect of context, some Jewish reactions have consisted of feigned ignorance and bafflement at what might have caused Black anti-Semitism. In a December 2019 article for the *Daily Beast*, Brooklyn-based Jay Michaelson attempts to explain the causes of "the new wave of anti-Semitic hate."[40] What his article in facts consists of is a series of mystifications of what is really a fairly straightforward story. For Michaelson, "speaking as a Jewish parent who lives in Brooklyn, I can tell you that it's terrifying. It is also confusing." The only thing Michaelson seems sure of is that "hate" is involved, but he courageously probes deeper by asking: "Hate, yes, but what kind of hate?" His conclusion? "The answer is not simple." Michaelson does concede that some of the anti-Jewish actions of recent decades contain "glimmers of ideology"—"the Crown Heights riot of 1991 was in part about city resources, housing, gentrification, policing and political power." But he follows this by insisting that "these attacks say nothing about African-Americans or anti-Semitism in Black communities. … To eradicate anti-Semitism, we must understand it—and right now, when it comes to this devastating new wave of attacks, we don't."

Other than blank confusion, then, does Michaelson suggest that anyone at all is blameworthy for the recent outbreaks of Black anti-Semitism? After much confusion, the fog settles and the real perpetrator comes into Michaelson's view: Donald Trump. Michaelson unveils the villain of the story as follows:

> While conspiracy-mongering exists on the left and the right, there is no left-wing or African-American equivalent of President Trump, who has freely traded in anti-Semitic stereotypes, sometimes in a joking way. … Indeed, Trump's contribution to our conspiracy-fevered culture is broader than specifically anti-Semitic conspiracies.

---

[40] Jay Michaelson, "What's Behind the New Wave of Anti-Semitic Hate?," *The Daily Beast* (December 31, 2019).
https://www.thedailybeast.com/whats-behind-the-new-wave-in-anti-semitic-hate

For example, regarding the 2016 election alone, Trump has claimed, baselessly, that it was rigged (even though he won anyway), that millions of people voted illegally in it, that Ukraine (not Russia) interfered with it, and that there are still important email servers floating around out there that we have to get our hands on. When you play with fire like this, vulnerable populations get burned. Especially Jews.

The real reason for Black attacks on Jews is thus unveiled with crystal clarity. According to Michaelson, it all began when Donald Trump made some jokes that some Jews perceived to refer to "canards" about Jews and money. The situation was compounded further when Trump complained about Hillary Clinton keeping state business on a private email server. Unable to control themselves in light of Trump's jokes, and rendered paranoid by talk of Ukrainian meddling and the security protocols of email servers, the Blacks of Brooklyn rose up in violence against the "vulnerable population" in their midst — the entirely innocent, passive and wealthy Hasidic landlords who owned their slums and debts. Right.

THE MATERIAL REACTION

It often pays to observe what Jews do rather than what they say. Steven Gold, writing on the Jewish response to growing Black anti-Semitism in 1940s Harlem, comments:

Being well organized, Jewish communal associations took note when Jewish merchants were accused of inappropriate behavior. When African-American journalists or activists complained about the exploitative behavior of ghetto merchants, Jewish spokesmen often resisted accepting responsibility and instead labeled accusers as anti-Semites for referring to the merchants' religion. Contending that Jewish merchants treated Blacks no worse than other Whites did, they objected to being singled out.[41]

Resisting accepting responsibility for exploitative and inappropriate behavior has long been the favored option of Jews, even when confronted with quite extreme and violent manifestations of anti-Semitism. In fact, one of the obvious themes of Jewish history is the persistence of negative behaviors amidst ever-intensifying efforts to entrench within the host

---

[41] Gold, *The Store in the Hood*, 75.

society, often via radically increased security and associated privileges (e.g., restricted freedoms for non-Jews, harsh penalties for anti-Semitism). A constant of Jewish history is that in general Jews do not change behavior that is seen negatively by non-Jews; rather, they find ways to continue to engage in the behavior but avoid the consequences. As such, one would expect that Black anti-Semitism will not significantly change patterns of Jewish behavior in Black areas, and that we will instead witness Jewish communities enjoying very high levels of police protection and the promotion of the idea that Jews are a vulnerable, passive, and special people entirely deserving of special treatment. Additionally, despite Jewish rhetoric blaming Black anti-Semitism on Whites, one would expect a high level of suspicion of Blacks among Jews, and subtle attempts by Jews to punish Blacks for their aggressions.

Security for Jews has already vastly increased since December 2019, with the *Guardian* reporting that police have stepped up patrols in "Borough Park, Midwood, Crown Heights, Bedford-Stuyvesant and Williamsburg, as well as establishing community-based neighborhood safety coalitions overseen by the Office for the Prevention of Hate Crimes. In addition, the city announced an increased NYPD presence at houses of worship and during local events. Six new surveillance towers and additional security cameras will be installed throughout the neighborhoods."[42] As well as increasing security on the ground, Jewish leaders last week successfully lobbied Attorney General William Barr to announce a "zero tolerance" policy for anti-Semitism at the federal level. The new, harsher approach to crimes against Jews will get its first trial in the case of Tiffany Harris, a Brooklyn-based Black woman of dubious mental health who slapped three Jewish women and now, on the orders of Barr, will face federal hate crime charges which carry a maximum of 30 years in prison.[43]

The issue of Jewish security has also called into question the putatively selfless Jewish interest in "social justice." Having previously backed New York's "no bail" criminal justice reforms, ostensibly intended to stop the injustice of those in poverty (mainly Blacks) spending more time in jail

---

[42] Edward, Helmore, "Jewish Groups Push Back against Police Surge in Wake of Antisemitic Attacks," *Guardian* (December 30, 2019).

https://www.theguardian.com/us-news/2019/dec/30/new-york-antisemitic-attacks-policing

[43] Lia Eustachewich, Reuven Fenton, Tina Moore and Bruce Golding, "Tiffany Harris Charged with Federal Hate Crimes in Anti-Semitic Attacks," *New York Post* (January 28, 2020).

https://nypost.com/2020/01/28/tiffany-harris-charged-with-federal-hate-crimes-in-anti-semitic-attacks/

than those with the funds to bail their way out (mainly Whites), Jews are now rapidly turning on the policy change and demanding that "hate crime" exemptions be considered. In other words, Jews want subtle protections and subtle punishments.

> People are panicking, people feel frightened," said Chaim Deutsch, a New York City councilman who represents a Brooklyn district with a large Hasidic population. "When they see someone like Tiffany Harris is released on bail, and got released only to go assault someone again, it sends the wrong message." Deutsch is circulating an open letter to [Governor Andrew] Cuomo criticizing the new criminal justice reforms. Simcha Eichenstein, a state assemblyman who also represents a Brooklyn district, plans to introduce legislation that would remove all hate crime charges from the list of crimes that judges cannot set bail for. Deutsch told the *Forward* he supports Eichenstein's legislation. Concern for the repercussions of the bail reforms is growing among politicians. Cuomo has said he wants to reconsider the rules. Even progressives like Andrea Stewart-Cousins, the New York State Senate majority leader, has signaled her willingness to look at the rules again.[44]

A policy change that has been the cause célèbre of liberal multiculturalists for years is thus forced into sharp revision solely because it has been deemed to negatively impact Jewish security.

This is the true Jewish reaction to Black anti-Semitism, devoid of rhetorical smoke and mirrors, and steeped in centuries of tradition: deny responsibility; entrench their position in the society; continue and intensify existing behaviors; increase privileges and protections; punish opponents.

What a vicious and endless circle.

Andrew Joyce has a Ph.D. in Jewish Studies and is a regular contributor to The Occidental Quarterly *and* The Occidental Observer. Talmud and Taboo, *a collection of his essays, is in preparation.*

---

[44] "Jews Say New York's Bail Reform Law Is Helping Anti-Semites," *Forward* (January 7, 2020).
https://forward.com/news/national/437905/new-york-bail-reform-antisemitic-hate-crimes/

THE NEW BOLSHEVISM IN THE LEGAL PROFESSION: THE EFFECT OF ACTIVIST LAW FACULTY ON STANDARDS OF JURISPRUDENCE, PROFESSIONAL CONDUCT, AND UNIVERSITY PEDAGOGY

V. S. SOLOVYEV

Political neutrality does not require the tower or the veil, but a commitment to honest discussion on the basis of reason and evidence. This commitment implies a commitment to truth beyond position or interest. An account of academic freedom for law schools that ignores our professional obligations must become either a platitude or a denial of responsibility.

J. Peter Byrne, "Academic Freedom and Political Neutrality in Law Schools: An Essay on Structure and Ideology in Professional Education"[1]

Colleges and universities are disciplinary, not political, institutions. They exist to serve the common good in the production and distribution of expert knowledge, as well as in the pedagogical inculcation of a mature independence of mind. Research and teaching are sites of critical thinking.

AAUP 2019 statement, "In Defense of Knowledge and Higher Education"[2]

The best way to motivate Constructive legal work is to paint pictures of the brave new worlds that may follow upon the failure of our present enterprise in liberal activism.

Bruce Ackerman, *Reconstructing American Law*[3]

---

[1] J. Peter Byrne, "Academic Freedom and Political Neutrality in Law Schools: An Essay on Structure and Ideology in Professional Education," *Journal of Legal Education* 43 (1993): 315–339, 339

[2] American Association of University Professors, "In Defense of Knowledge and Higher Education" (November, 2019).
https://www.aaup.org/report/defense-knowledge-and-higher-education

[3] Bruce Ackerman, *Reconstructing American Law* (Harvard University Press, 1984), 103.

The great object of my fear is the federal judiciary. That body, like gravity, ever acting with noiseless foot and unalarming advance, is gaining ground step by step. … Let the eye of vigilance never be closed.
Thomas Jefferson, Letter to Spencer Roane[4]

He who controls the present, controls the past. He who controls the past, controls the future.
George Orwell, *1984*[5]

A juridico-civil (political) state is the relation of human beings to each other inasmuch as they stand jointly under public juridical laws (which are all coercive laws). An ethico-civil state is one in which they are united under laws without being coerced, i.e., under laws of virtue alone. Now, just as the rightful (but not therefore always righteous) state of nature, i.e., the juridical state of nature, is opposed to the first, so is the ethical state of nature distinguished from the second. In these two [states of nature] each individual prescribes the law to himself, and there is no external law to which he, along with the others, acknowledges himself to be subject. In both each individual is his own judge, and there is no effective public authority with power to determine legitimately, according to laws, what is in given cases the duty of each individual, and to bring about the universal execution of those laws. In an already existing political community all the political citizens are, as such, still in the ethical state of nature … . [W]oe to the legislator who would want to bring about through coercion a polity directed to ethical ends! For he would thereby not only achieve the very opposite of ethical ends, but also undermine his political ends and render them insecure. – The citizen of the political community therefore remains, so far as the latter's lawgiving authority is concerned, totally free: he may wish to enter with his fellow citizens into an ethical union over and above the political one.
Emmanuel Kant, *Religion Within the Boundaries of Mere Reason*[6]

In every system of morality, which I have hitherto met with, I have always remarked, that the author proceeds for some time in the ordinary way of reasoning, and establishes the being of a God, or makes observations concerning human affairs; when of a sudden I am surprised to find, that instead of the usual copulations of propositions, is, and is not, I meet with no proposition that is not

---

[4] Letter from Thomas Jefferson to Spencer Roane, March 9, 1821.
https://founders.archives.gov/documents/Jefferson/98-01-02-1900
[5] George Orwell, *1984*, Part One, Chapter 3.
[6] Emmanuel Kant, *Religion Within the Boundaries of Mere Reason*, in *Kant: Religion within the Boundaries of Mere Reason: And Other Writings* (Cambridge: Cambridge University Press, 1998; originally published: 1793), 6: 95–96.

connected with an ought, or an ought not. This change is imperceptible; but is, however, of the last consequence. For as this ought, or ought not, expresses some new relation or affirmation, it is necessary that it should be observed and explained; and at the same time that a reason should be given, for what seems altogether inconceivable, how this new relation can be a deduction from others, which are entirely different from it. ... This small attention would ... let us see that the distinction of vice and virtue is not founded merely on the relations of objects, nor is perceived by reason.

David Hume, *A Treatise of Human Nature*[7]

Bolshevism embraces anarchism in theory and totalitarianism in practice. In order to survive, the Bolshevist state must obliterate the potentially destabilizing forces inherent in democracy through a party dictatorship that is presented as the political self-determination of a free people.

Hans Kelsen, "Platonic Justice"[8]

ABSTRACT

There is an especially visible commonality in the current U.S. political economy that is defined by an ethno-religious and state special interest that is advanced largely through the re-casting and re-purposing of law. The modern university law school sits in its organizational center, acting as an asserted professional authority on legal interpretation; as an activism network node; and as an ideological pedagogic institution among students in captive degree programs. Four parallel but interrelated events bring these aspects into relief:

1. The White House Executive Order of December 11, 2019 extending Title VI to a specific re-interpretation of discrimination based on a singular identity of a person and a state, preceded by extensive state and federal legislation, and credentialed through media and other channels, by sympathetic university law faculty, especially at the universities of Chicago, Yale and Harvard.

2. The U.S. House of Representatives impeachment trial of 2019, which sought, and continues to pursue, an operational authority over foreign policy favorable to this identity and its corresponding interests, including a "Neo-Bolshevism" that seeks consolidation in U.S. bi-lateral relationships, and extending from its resource base in the U.S., *ipso facto*, threatens U.S. Constitutional law by normalizing

---

[7] David Hume, *A Treatise of Human Nature* (London: John Noon, 1738), 335.

[8] Hans Kelsen, "Platonic Justice," *Ethics* 48, no. 3 (April, 1938): 367–400, 1–2.

the interruption and capture of government, creating a tiered construct, one notionally public, the other private.

3. The concurrent announcement by the U.S. Executive Office of a Middle East "Deal of the Century" geopolitical plan concerning Palestine and Israel, without Palestinian representation.

4. The increasingly aggressive appropriation and eventual re-selling of U.S. intellectual and other property, developed within the university complex, that bypasses U.S. export and other legal restrictions through common academic practices of inter-university cooperation.

The explicit law-and-order suppression of criticism, dissent or information, either defining or exposing these issues, is central to their continued cultural embedding in U.S. institutions. Suppression is particularly important as the character of these institutions becomes further radicalized, thus requiring general social normalization and especially, cognitive surrender and infantilization, most recently seen in its "pre-takeover" phase by the virus and "pandemic" narratology with immediate state-level decrees involving social isolation, quarantine, economic shutdowns, and other experiments in controlling behavior. Suppression is also critical to the new "ideological iron square" on U.S. campuses, composed of interlocking narratives on terror, race, climate change, and security. These narratives which must be propagated, consolidated and thereby intergenerationally perpetuated, through the modern university. I assert that this effectively amounts to a "Neo-Bolshevism" which is implicitly codified through the modern law school. This Neo-Bolshevism includes a systematic but insidious anarchical assault on constitutional principles and law which is incrementally advanced under various identitarian and national security pretexts, but is structurally organized around what is in effect a third party in the American political economy — a party dedicated to social justice, judicial activism and economic redistribution.

INTRODUCTION

Where the law is backward, it must be made to seem progressive. Where the law is uncertain or permissive, it must be made to seem definite and mandatory. Where arguments are limited and honestly debatable, they must be made to seem comprehensive and inescapable. Where opponents refuse to yield, their positions must be distorted or they themselves must be belittled and insulted.

Robert F. Nagel, *The Implosion of American Federalism*[9]

The 'critical legal studies' strategy of self-revolutionizing legal reform proceeds on undefended assumptions. The liberals and free-market right-wingers have no right to complain since they generally proceed on similar assumptions. I regret the clumsy reference to "free-market right-wingers," but whatever these Chicago school chaps may be, conservatives they are not. … The most discouraging feature of the story of [Critical Legal Studies] so far emerges from its inadvertent revelation of the condition of the American Left as a whole. For it shows the extent to which the flower of the left-wing intelligentsia perceives the need for a political agenda attuned to the realities of a corporate state for which it has little stomach, and the extent to which it is unwilling to shed its utopian egalitarianism and destructive view of authority. The ability of a largely deranged Left to contribute to, much less lead, a political movement appropriate to the corporatism it woos and fears remains, to say the least, doubtful.

Eugene D. Genovese, "Critical Legal Studies as Radical Politics and World View"[10]

The form taken by the law, on the one hand, and by the legal system, on the other, are related, and both are central to the Rule of Law. Most theorists accept that the majority of laws will be aimed at meeting particular purposes, even if usually they can be framed in general terms, thereby falling equitably on all, be settled, well-known and clear. However, what prevents such laws being the purely personal orders of officials or rulers derives as much (if not more) from the manner in which they are enacted, implemented and systemised than from the form they take. Indeed, it is this latter feature that gets around the paradox that laws are necessarily made and enforced by persons by insisting that they do so in legal ways that are consistent and impartial. There are no universal truths of reason that stand outside any construction and can serve as a criterion. Instead, we must relate our concerns to those of others in more particular ways through an on-going process of public dialogue.

Thus, the Rule of Law emerges from the exercise of practical rather than theoretical reason, the product of a politics where all oblige each other to 'hear the other side'. For arbitrary power can only be blocked through the equalisation of power, and achieving this condition is a matter not of principle but of continuous

---

[9] Robert F. Nagel, *The Implosion of American Federalism* (New York: Oxford University Press, 2002), 174, 177.

[10] Eugene D. Genovese, "Critical Legal Studies as Radical Politics and World View," *Yale Journal of Law and Humanities* 3, no. 1 (1991): 131–156, 140, 156.

political vigilance and struggle. Indeed, it is the Hobbesian desire to overcome all struggles for power that represents the chief danger to the Rule of Law, for it leads ineluctably to the arbitrary rule of some persons over the rest.

Richard Bellamy, "The Rule of Law and the Rule of Persons"[11]

The mark of Platonic philosophy is a radical dualism. The Platonic world is not one of unity; and the abyss which in many ways results from this bifurcation appears in innumerable forms.

Hans Kelsen, "Platonic Justice"[12]

There are several current interrelated events in American politics that are teasing out of the American multiculturalism matrix a special-interest advocacy that seeks, on the one hand, to ratify a presidential executive order, and on the other hand, to dismantle constitutional law: White House free speech advocacy and accommodating conservative speech; protecting against anti-Semitism in university environments; the Muslim travel ban; the "Deal of the Century" concerning the U.S.-Israel carve-out of Palestine; and the impeachment trial, serving both as a domestic distraction, and as foreign policy advocacy especially concerning Ukraine as the "base-camp" of a neo-Bolshevism directed at the Former Soviet Union. At the core, or node from which these spokes extend, lies a special-interest, bi-lateral ideological commonality among the U.S. and Israel. Its most recent flowering is the so-called "Covid-19" pandemic which resulted in a de facto U.S. martial law and an unprecedented private, special-interest withdrawal from the U.S. Treasury, of over $2 Trillion dollars, carefully orchestrated by White House advisor Jared Kushner and Treasury Secretary Steven Mnuchin.

Let me explain.

On December 11, 2019, the White House issued a "Law and Order" Executive Order, or "EO" that asserted Title VI Civil Rights Act protection to certain university students and others,[13] who are thereby interpreted

---

[11] Richard Bellamy, "The Rule of Law and the Rule of Persons," in Preston King (ed.), *Trusting in Reason: Martin Hollis and The Philosophy of Social Action* (Routledge, 2003), 222, 247.

[12] Hans Kelsen, "Platonic Justice," *Ethics* 48, no. 3 (April, 1938): 367–400, 367.

[13] Executive Order on Combating Anti-Semitism (December 11, 2019).

https://www.whitehouse.gov/presidential-actions/executive-order-combating-anti-semitism.

It is important to realize however, that this EO had precedent and preparation going back to at least 2017; indeed, the Trump administration, largely through Trump's son-in-law, dual citizen Jared Kushner, almost immediately after assuming office began an broadly as a special case, or carve out, subject to Federal judgement and adjudication, including an ex-ante threat of financial discriminatory treatment (withholding) against any higher education institution, public or private, deemed in violation. Interestingly, this only applies to a contested discrimination—under vague standards of evidence and adjudication, leaving open effective ex-post-facto intervention and constitutional violation.[14] This has several fascinating ramifications.

The other event involves the impeachment action brought by the Democratic party in the U.S. House of Representatives and organized by a small faction of special interests within it, financially underwritten or encouraged, by systematic external support, some foreign. It has two dimensions worth noting.

First, while it may appear to be generated from normal or conventional Congressional rules, rights, obligations or procedure, it follows none. It is rather a subversion, directed not merely at overthrowing an elected president, but also, as I will argue, at a deeper level, it aims to *normalize* such extreme action by effectively dismantling the U.S. Constitution. Second, that objective is greatly aided by a tightly organized and managed network of congressional advocates, supported by an ideologically complementary group of activist university law professors. In both cases—congressional and academic—the network is nearly culturally and socially homogenous. If such a network were comprised primarily or exclusively of any otherwise concentrated group, it would likely be perceived as unusual, compromised by intention, or motivated by factors irrelevant to the stated cause of action.

This network has been especially visible for the previous two decades in recent political phenomena, including the incubation, dissemination

---

explicit campaign of anti-Semitism activism and re-interpretation. This included a quietly instituted 2018 "Beta" version of the 2019 EO, issued through the U.S. Department of Education, which as *Haaretz* reported, for the first time, used the U.S. State Department's definition of anti-Semitism which equates it with "anti-Israel" criticism. Moreover, this was preceded by the "Anti-Semitism Awareness Act" and several acts by states that financially penalize companies (reaching down even into their pensions) that participate directly or indirectly in any form of BDS activity. The federal Congressional version stalled, which explains the EO. See: S.852–Anti-Semitism Awareness Act of 2019.

https://www.congress.gov/bill/116th-congress/senate-bill/852/text

[14] Ex-post-facto violation is normally thought by the legal academy as only applying to criminal law; however, in principle, and especially in current jurisprudence surrounding the establishment of the Patriot Act and the Department of Justice's Manual of War intervention in civil law, it is extended into civil law. For an alternative perspective, see: William W. Crosskey, "True Meaning of the Constitutional Prohibition of Ex-Post-Facto Laws," *University of Chicago Law Review* 14, no. 4 (1947): 539–565.

and operationalization of the Global War on Terror (GWOT). A fascinating central theme in the impeachment opening statements is a tortured interpretation of constitutional law, reinforced by equally misleading assertions by sympathetic academics, including Laurence Tribe, Cass Sunstein, Nikolas Bowie and Noah Feldman of Harvard; Pamela Karlan of Stanford; Harold Koh and Bruce Ackerman of Yale;[15] Michael Gerhardt of the University of North Carolina, Ronald Krotoszynski of the University of Alabama; Kate Shaw of Yeshiva University;[16] and Tom Ginsburg, Eric Posner and Aziz Huq of the University of Chicago, among many others. However, in addition there is a structural constellation of larger geopolitical interests and positions that rest on the Ukraine as a proxy for an historical ethnic struggle—or historical contestation for resources and power—with, and within, the former Soviet Union, and still, the current Russian state and its leadership.[17]

Indeed, the impeachment hearing and Senate trial are centered in specifically ethno-religious positions among U.S. House members (notably

---

[15] Koh, a former Obama State Department employee, wrote "A National Security Impeachment," seemingly unaware of opposing evidence—unsurprising at Yale (called "a 14th Amendment club with a registrar").

Harold Hongju Koh, "A National Security Impeachment," Yale MacMillan Center (December 17, 2019).

https://macmillan.yale.edu/news/harold-hongju-koh-national-security-impeachment

These examples do not include the "infamous 500" law professors who collectively signed a conviction solidarity public letter, with no due diligence over evidence or evidence standards, including even elementary chain-of-custody standards:

"Hundreds of Law Profs Declare Trump's Conduct 'Clearly Impeachable,'" *Law.com* (December 6, 2019).

https://www.law.com/nationallawjournal/2019/12/06/hundreds-of-law-profs-declare-trumps-conduct-clearly-impeachable/?slreturn=20200025170031

[16] Shaw wrote an especially trying example as it is so flawed by severe partisanship that it requires a wholesale intellectual correction before the issues raised can even be coherently debated:

Kate Shaw, "Why Trump's Lawyers Should Talk Like Lawyers," *New York Times* (January 28, 2020).

https://www.nytimes.com/2020/01/28/opinion/trump-impeachment-trial.html

[17] Rob Urie, "Impeachment Brought to You by the CIA," *Counterpunch* (October 4, 2019).

https://www.counterpunch.org/2019/10/04/impeachment-brought-to-you-by-the-cia/

Scott Uhelinger, "Ukraine Is the Canary in the Coal Mine for Intel Coimmunity," *Newsmax* (September 30, 2019).

https://www.newsmax.com/scottuehlinger/intelligence-community-cia-politicization/2019/09/30/id/934950/

Adam Schiff and Jerry Nadler), House witnesses, including military witnesses and Ukrainian assets. If President Trump had made a "phone call" to New Zealand, Ireland, China, Japan or Germany, would such interests and contentions even be present? As House witness Ambassador Taylor stated, "Ukraine is on the front line" of the current contention. *But why Ukraine? What interests, objectives and operations were being threatened?*[18]

---

[18] Cf., Victoria Nuland's sub-rosa actions in Ukraine in her role as former Ambassador:

Robert Perry, "The Mess that Nuland Made," *Consortium News* (July 13, 2015).

https://consortiumnews.com/2015/07/13/the-mess-that-nuland-made/

The complexity of Ukraine as a "front-line" in geopolitical contestation is also evident in the recent U.S. drone strike against Iran's military personnel, but which was followed immediately by an airline accident anomaly. As an aerospace and defense expert, it was brought to my attention that a number of circumstantial elements raise questions as to the origin and cause of the fatal shoot-down of the Ukraine International Airlines plane in Tehran. It was the only departure that evening in the early dusk period, among nearly a dozen departures, that was identified by Iran radar and electronic signaling, to be "coded" as an enemy target.

Ukraine International Airlines is controlled by Israeli citizen Aron Mayberg, in partnership with triple citizen (Ukraine-Israel-Cyprus) billionaire Ihor Kolomoyskyi, through a number of off-shore entities. Iran's Parliament had previously moved to block their operations from Iranian airspace due to concerns over possible decoy black operations. The avionics on the Ukrainian aircraft may also have been contaminated, and that would be difficult without cooperation, or if it was an Iranian flag carrier. The ownership and control of Ukrainian Airlines is an important potential independent variable, as the plane may have been "prepped" beforehand in a number of ways. There are many possibilities and permutations of motive and means; this is one. However, the possibility of outside, external signal and/or cyber interference, and certainly, the coordination with media at the *New York Times* in particular, is significant. Indeed, the *Times* continues to publish propaganda concerning the shoot down, now calling it a "cover-up."

Farnaz Fassihi, "Anatomy of a Lie: How Iran Covered Up the Downing of an Airliner," *New York Times* (January 26, 2020).

https://www.nytimes.com/2020/01/26/world/middleeast/iran-plane-crash-coverup.html.

The use of civil aircraft has been a hallmark of the GWOT, which may leave strong evidence of origin and expertise. The activist dissemination of video taken by what claimed to be a bystander is also not feasible, as he was, at 6:00 AM on a pitch-black morning standing in a largely abandoned ghetto of Tehran, with his camera pointed *directly at the point of origin* of the two missiles *well before they were launched*, and following them precisely to their point of impact. *This highly suggests foreknowledge and planning* which would survive evidence standards in third-party forum. The Iran government is investigating the accident precisely on these grounds of cyber and intelligence warfare, including Israel's potential role in the event by "ghosting" the transponder signal through cyber attack, or preparing the aircraft software prior to departure through cooperation with airline ownership. See:

THE FOURTH ESTATE OR IS IT THE FIFTH COLUMN? THE ELITE LAW SCHOOL NETWORK IN MEDIA PUBLIC RELATIONS

Mundus vult decipi: the world wants to be deceived. The truth is too complex and frightening; the taste for the truth is an acquired taste that few acquire. Not all deceptions are palatable. Untruths are too easy to come by, too quickly exploded, too cheap and ephemeral to give lasting comfort. Mundus vult decipi; but there is a hierarchy of deceptions. Near the bottom of the ladder is journalism: a steady stream of irresponsible distortions that most people find refreshing although on the morning after, or at least within a week, it will be stale and flat. On a higher level we find fictions that men eagerly believe, regardless of the evidence, because they gratify some wish. Near the top of the ladder we encounter curious mixtures of untruth and truth that exert a lasting fascination on the intellectual community. What cannot, on the face of it, be wholly true, although it is plain that there is some truth in it, evokes more discussion and dispute, divergent exegeses and attempts at emendations than what has been stated very carefully, without exaggeration or one-sidedness. The Book of Proverbs is boring compared to the Sermon on the Mount.

Martin Buber, *I and Thou*, trans. by Walter Kaufmann (Scribner Classics, 2000)

University of Chicago Law's Tom Ginsburg asserts that impeachment is "good for democracy."[19] This is an interesting example of dissimulation that may be worth some brief additional treatment.

Chicago law professors Aziz Huq and Tom Ginsburg try to convince the public, for example, that impeachment is good for a democracy like the U.S., comparing the U.S. to South American and other third-world regimes; they claim that it helps "reset" order by washing out corruption, *and should be effectively normalized*, while ignoring the profound wisdom of the Federalist, among other documents, concerning the need for bipartisan consensus for such an action. Their argument cites data and statistics, *but it is little more than critical legal studies, masquerading as law and*

Philip Giraldi, "Ukraine Airlines Flight 752: Iran Shot It Down, but There May Be More to the Story," *The Unz Review* (January 15, 2020).

https://www.sott.net/article/427485-Ukraine-Airlines-Flight-752-Iran-shot-it-down-but-there-may-be-more-to-the-story

[19] Tom Ginsburg, Aziz Huq and David Landau, "Opinion: Impeachment Has Rebooted Other Democracies Stuck in Corruption and Gridlock," *Los Angeles Times* (December 15, 2019).

https://www.latimes.com/opinion/story/2019-12-15/impeachment-democracy-presidents-donald-trump *economics.*[20] Worse, they seek to re-define impeachment as an instrument of an effective congressional political party, thereby bypassing the relevant constitutional clause entirely. Their argument is in reality one seeking to uproot current U.S. constitutional design by making the president subject to the House serving at its pleasure through the risk of a no-confidence vote. *It is a coy argument for repurposing the Constitution to a political ideology, and an entirely different standard in separation.*[21] It is legalistic

---

[20] But it is worse than that: it is irresponsible legal fabrication, and inexplicable detachment from the core principles of U.S. government construction, that clearly set out the standards for impeachment. They include Madison's clear thinking concerning separation of powers such that the chief executive was not answerable strictly to the House (as an effective parliament) but part of three co-equal branches (moreover, Federalist 65 clearly outlines the danger of such proceedings on partisan lines). He devoted much thought to impeachment standards, and the convention debated whether it was even a sound idea. George Mason proposed a standard of "mal-administration" but the framers, Madison in particular, fought to establish a much higher cause based in English common law (treason and high crimes standard). "Obstruction of Congress and abuse of power," are perhaps merely mal-administration but that would apply to every president in modern history so accused. Huq and Ginsburg never find their bearings in the most fundamental, relevant guideline — the impeachment clause of the constitution; indeed, they ignore it entirely. But more inexplicably, they seek to redefine impeachment as an effective congressional party "golden share" in pubic elections. Their argument is inherently flawed by the most basic basis of legal reasoning, evidence, and standards.

Ginsburg, Huq and Landau, "Opinion: Impeachment Has Rebooted Other Democracies Stuck in Corruption and Gridlock." See also: Adam Bonica, Adam S. Chilton and Maya Sen, "The Political Ideologies of American Lawyers," Coase-Sandor Working Paper Series in Law and Economics No. 732 (2015); James C. Phillips, "Political Discrimination and Law Professor Hiring," *New York University Journal of Law and Liberty* 12 (2019): 560–617.

[21] It may be provocative to consider if by such legal political activism by academics in which law professors are effectively defined by federal character as employees (e.g., a law professor who is also a judge) or agent, such that the Hatch Act is applicable. Indeed, the White House 11 December, 2918 EO tying political compliance in Title VI application subject to funding determination, recasts entirely the nature of the university (public and private) and the nature of its employees. This is constructively reinforced when law professors serve on federal investigation panels. See for example, Lynn Sweet, "Stone's Experience on Intelligence Panel: Chicago Sun Times," University of Chicago Law School (December 25, 2013).

https://www.law.uchicago.edu/news/stones-experience-intelligence-panel-chicago-sun-times

This would also apply in the event professors act as consultants to government interests, work as judges, or are paid with federal funds to advise election candidates or their interests, among other acts that transform their identity.

Avram Goldstein, "Teacher to Lose Job under Hatch Act," *The Washington Post* (April 15, 2002).

deception, which "invites a willing suspension of disbelief so that, if we but accede to a creative reformulation of language, reality can be altered and improved. "In order to mandate progress in the name of law, especially constitutional law, it is necessary to deceive."[22]

What Huq and Ginsberg embrace is nothing that can be identified with common law, but rather with a certain variation of a (very slight) kind of natural law, but one that can reflect a modern bourgeois political sentiment of public justice, that can purport to justify on moral or ideological grounds, a dismantling of constitutional law, *where they ignore its internal moral power, and seek to impose from the outside, their own moral standard.* It is actually a separation of law and morality, more in a spirit of radical positivism.

There is another interesting historical context in current progressive (I would call neo-Bolshevik) efforts to interpret legal tradition in effectively "social-revolutionary" ways that ultimately rest on the broader context of Hegel's philosophy, to the extent it may be seen as embracing a "liberation" theology. It shares a fascinating similarity with contention over a German religious constitution, and may appear enlightened, but merely seeks to replace what it considers one religion (a U.S. constitution founded in many ways on non-secular morality) with its own (a secular radical dismantling):

> Modern projects to supply constitutional orders with supervening normative philosophical or theoretical foundations often take their lead from the way in which Kantian and Hegelian philosophies contested the legitimacy of the German constitution in the nominated period. The intellectual weaponry deployed by the early nineteenth-century idealists would be used in other places and times and for other purposes — for example, in the political philosophies of John Rawls and Jürgen Habermas.[23]

Professors Huq and Ginsburg are thus by no means alone in selective or deceptive interpretation standards.[24]

---

https://www.washingtonpost.com/archive/politics/2002/04/15/teacher-to-lose-job-under-hatch-act/8dc9ced8-5996-41da-a898-5837958f1459/.

[22] Nagel, "Lies and Nationhood," 174, 177.

[23] Ian Hunter, "Public Law and the Limits of Philosophy: German Idealism and the Religious Constitution," *Critical Inquiry* 44, no. 3 (Spring 2018): 528–553.

[24] Other recent media lobbying by law professors is often not quite as carefully disguised. Often it is mere raw partisanship that is so unstable in law, general reasoning, and the management of facts, that it is difficult to respond to, as it demands a wholesale intellectual rescue:

Harvard Law's Cass Sunstein, formerly at Chicago Law for many years and an Obama staff appointee, reliably provides highly partisan and ideologically based legal and administrative interpretations that are usually cloaked in a seemingly fair-minded proposition. But as you unpack the details, they are either very deconstructionist, or just poorly reasoned. An example is his *New York Times* op-ed, "Imagine That Donald Trump Has Almost No Control Over Justice: Congress should transform the department into an independent agency untouched by the president's whims."[25]

Sunstein bases his argument on what seems to be a reasonable comparison to other independent agencies. Unfortunately, he leaves out the most important details: Was the Department of Justice (DoJ) independent under President Obama and, assuming the obvious, did Sunstein object to Obama's influence? Who appoints DoJ personnel? If not appointed, and representing "the public" as Sunstein opines, are they instead elected, and by whom and under what conditions? To whom does the DoJ report to? But that's just the proverbial low-hanging objections. Sunstein's actual argument isn't about an independent DoJ, or an institutional organizational proposal that necessarily must include many other complex government design problems and solutions, but is merely an objection to *Trump* having executive influence or authorities over the Department of Justice (indeed, his article title, if in earnest, would have used the noun "president" rather than naming the president, thereby of course already eroding any legitimacy to his argument. Of course, his argument is functioning as "red meat" for the *Times* readership, so that one has to fill in much of its context. Its purpose is to emotionally trigger them and reinforce their bias.

His hypocrisy is too obvious to labor over, suffice it to say that his previous chief executive took "influence" and "control" to new levels of mendacity (with his right-hand man political operative, Eric Holder as Attorney General) which is instead what much of the current White House is trying to unwind, and correct. "Control" is an interesting term because Sunstein doesn't actually think through what this means, and in what many different ways "control" is effected. He confuses executive line responsibility with organizational re-alignment, the latter of which the previous administration rather mendaciously instituted over its two terms. That is, it re-aligned several agencies, departments and bureaus, with a network of party ideological "assets" or institutional loyalists, who would

---

[25] Cass Sunstein, "Imagine that Donald Trump Has Almost No Control Over Justice," *New York Times* (February 20, 2020).

https://www.nytimes.com/2020/02/20/opinion/sunday/trump-barr-justice-department.html

provide a reliable cultural and even operational resistance function to oppose executive office and other authority.

Moreover, as a law professor, Sunstein leaves out the profound legal changes codified in the Patriot Act, which grants the executive office broad, nearly unlimited privilege and authority over the entire government infrastructure.[26] The U.S. president now *is* the Department of Justice. Surely Sunstein is well-versed in the Act, as former head of the Office of Information and Regulatory Affairs, perhaps the essence of unelected, unaccountable regulatory reach in the former administration.[27] He is a perfect example of what political bias, ideology, and special interests do to rational thought and professional cognitive integrity: they it undermine them, unless they are very carefully managed. Such care is rarely observed.

Harvard Law's unfortunate professor Laurence Tribe, provides a nearly textbook-perfect case of interpretive deception and cognitive confusion in his recent *Washington Post* op-ed. As a legal scholar citing the Federalist papers, his entire argument rests on selectively ignoring its

---

[26] See Michiko Kakutani, "Unchecked and Unbalanced," *New York Times* (July 6, 2007).

https://www.nytimes.com/2007/07/06/books/06book.html

Elizabeth Goitein, "The Alarming Scope of Presidential Emergency Powers," *The Atlantic* (January/February, 2019).

https://www.theatlantic.com/magazine/archive/2019/01/presidential-emergency-powers/576418/

[27] The 1976 National Emergencies Act laid the modern foundation of effectively extra-constitutional presidential powers containing over 130 statutory provisions," citing Goitein, "The Alarming Scope of Presidential Emergency Powers."

See also: "Guide to Emergency Powers and Their Use," Brennan Center (April 24, 2020).

https://www.brennancenter.org/our-work/research-reports/guide-emergency-powers-and-their-use

This was reinforced by subsequent administrations, through additional Acts and Executive Orders, such as the 1977 International Emergency Economic Powers Act, and Executive Order 13224 under the Bush administration, among others. The consolidation of modern presidential authority, however, was finally codified in the 2003 U.S. Patriot Act. As former head of OIRA (Office of Information and Regulatory Affairs) under the previous administration, surely the professor appreciates this legal complexity and its ramifications. Sunstein seems to ignore the powerful legal umbrella of special acts and orders that make his proposal legally moot and inert. To expect Congress, moreover, to go back and unwind such authorities they previously ratified, is politically unrealistic. Sunstein may object to the current president's executive latitude, but it will take a more complicated and comprehensive restructuring of those presidential authorities than the simple one he recommends, if his proposal is to have any "teeth" going forward.

most relevant sections, while building his case on a patchwork of historical anecdote and casual personal opinions.

> The issue of natural right presents itself today as a matter of party
> allegiance. Looking around us, we see two hostile camps, heavily
> fortified and guarded. One is occupied by the liberals of various de-
> scriptions, the other by the Catholic and non-Catholic disciples of
> Thomas Aquinas.[28]

Moreover, Sunstein carefully confuses the reader (and students) by
misinterpreting constitutional and other language: an impeachment
crime may not necessarily be *per se* statutorily criminal or indictable, but
rather a "high crime," a term borrowed from English common law. That
is, he confuses *crime* with *criminal*. As does University of Missouri Law's
Frank Bowman, who appeals to "The almost universal consensus — in
Great Britain, in the colonies, in the American states between 1776 and
1787, at the Constitutional Convention and since" in his argument against
a *per se* criminal threshold, *yet doesn't seem to realize that he thereby precisely
ratifies the Federalist concept of bi-partisan consensus in making impeachment
determination.*[29] Such a crime, or act, or transgression, is defined, and contrasted with, mere mal-administration, *through Federalist 65's most sound
test: bi-partisan consensus in the presence of relevant evidence and evidence
standards. Bi-partisanship—and consensus—is the fail-safe impeachment standard—*a standard that transgresses mere historical interpretation and linguistic debate. *It is the surest, perhaps only, way to determine "how high is
high" in judging, regardless of the semantics deployed.* That is precisely why,
among other reasons, there is separation: the executive office does not fall
under general House authority, let alone the attitudes of one party, as it
otherwise would in a "parliamentarian" structure (and why the Founders
altered the U.S. model away from the British model). Mr. Tribe apparently
either doesn't understand that, or deliberately ignores the fundamental
independent variables in the entire impeachment equation. *To make his
argument, he must dismantle the entire intellectual foundation of American*

---

[28] Leo Strauss, *Natural Right and History* (Chicago: University of Chicago Press,
1953), 7.

[29] Charlie Savage, "'Constitutional Nonsense': Trump's Impeachment Defense Defies
Legal Consensus," *New York Times* (January 20, 2020).
    https://www.nytimes.com/2020/01/20/us/politics/trump-impeachment-legal-
defense.html

constitutional law.[30] To paraphrase the response of a White House counsel to the Senate,[31] Mr. Tribe carves out constitutional accommodation, contempt and litigation as too intellectually and factually inconvenient for his politically driven motivations (yet implicitly embraces subjective intent, which surely he knows is a deficient basis).

Further vitiating his argument, Mr. Tribe avoids a discussion of evidence standards, an omission that undermines his entire position and his general credibility.[32] Like too many legal arguments, it is in a cognitive fog regarding the necessary distinctions among, and active management of, dependent, independent and control variables.[33] *Ultimately, one has to ask why Mr. Tribe is teaching in a law school* and not rather working as a commercial lobbyist and consultant.[34] Like other academics, he wants to

---

[30] See the excellent *Novus Ordo Seclorum: The Intellectual Origins of the Constitution*, by the late University of Alabama historian Forrest McDonald (Lawrence, KS: University of Kansas Press, 1985).

[31] "Trial Memorandum of President Donald J. Trump" (January 20, 2020).

https://www.whitehouse.gov/wp-content/uploads/2020/01/Trial-Memorandum-of-President-Donald-J.-Trump.pdf

[32] Laurence Tribe, "Trump's Lawyers Should Not Be Allowed to Use Bogus Legal Arguments on Impeachment," *Washington Post* (January 9, 2020).

https://www.washingtonpost.com/opinions/2020/01/19/trumps-lawyers-shouldnt-be-allowed-use-bogus-legal-arguments-impeachment/

[33] For a discussion of various types of variables, see: Riti Gupta, "What Are Dependent, Independent, and Controlled Variables?," *Sciencing* (February 10, 2020).

https://sciencing.com/dependent-independent-controlled-variables-8360093.html

I am not suggesting, nor strictly following, the logic of the argument made by Jensen in "The Nature of Legal Argument." That is, poor or deceptive legal reasoning in my view is not necessarily a product of a violation of rules of logic, *but rather the embrace or deployment of logical fallacy, and especially, the difficulty in discerning its presence.*

O. C. Jensen, *The Nature of Legal Argument* (Oxford: Basil Blackwell, 1957).

[34] Tribe has immediately found a new Constitutional law issue to re-interpret after the Senate trial, concerning the White House-led intervention in air travel security privileges:

Laurence Tribe, "Trump's Policy on New York's 'Trusted Travelers' is Unconstitutional," *New York Times* (February 14, 2020).

In this instance, a fundamental bias is brought into relief concerning the radical activism of Tribe (and Judge Richard Posner of the U.S. Court of Appeals) in upending Constitutional rights on the basis of "national security" emanating from the GWOT. Otherwise Tribe invokes equity, fairness and due process in his criticism of recent White House policy that universally blocks all New York air travelers from participation in a federal "Trusted Traveler" program, a program that, as anyone going through LaGuardia or Kennedy airports on a regular basis can attest, is very convenient. Mr. Tribe is right to call upon these fundamental legal principles. He may not, however, have consulted the 2003 U.S Patriot Act, enacted after 911, that gave precisely the executive powers he decries, to the chief executive. It created an effective extra-constitutional authority give advice (and take payment) but not be held accountable or liable — effective professorial immunity. There are several productive philosophical arguments or inquiries that can be made around special-interest legal activism. They include the more obvious CLS (critical legal studies) element; a "radical legal positivism" (and the less obvious but fascinating issue of philosophical hermeneutics, and a "hermeneutics of suspicion" *that the legal activist mode should immediately provoke*.[35]

ACCOUNTABILITY: WHERE ARE THE MODEL RULES OF PROFESSIONAL CONDUCT?

The Attorney Registration and Disciplinary Committee (ARDC) hosts the so-called Model Rules for Professional Conduct, with the ability to sanction through attorney registration and license privileges. Many of the ARDC's "model rules of professional conduct" are fairly straightforward, based in a code of ethics, equity and liability, and focused on the effective legal fiduciary obligations generated when lawyers provide commercially based (compensated) third-party services to clients (individuals or various entities). *At no time since the House impeachment or since the Senate trial procedures began, has even one academic law professor raised one of the most glaring legal violations involving House Manager Adam Schiff* who by such rules is disqualified in his role in the Senate trial, because he is a fact witness.[36]

I discuss these particular cases of law school professor political lobbying and bias, because they are good examples not only of legal infirmity, but pedagogic dishonesty by advancing arguments in the public domain that are specifically concocted to advance an activist agenda which is

---

with very broad interpretative flexibility. Mr. Tribe cites case law concerning state rights upheld by the Supreme Court, and claims that such cases may not be very convincing in this context   He's right. He then finally turns to legal philosophy in the Constitution. He's right again. For example, certain laws can't be made "after the fact" (ex post facto); however, he is wrong when he interprets ex ante procedures (a charge made on prediction or before the fact) as unconstitutional. That is precisely what the Patriot Act now allows or encourages, based on "societal protection" principles. Normal rule of law, and the U.S. Constitution, were turned on their head after September, 2001. Many lawyers and law professors, including Mr. Tribe, made little if any objections in Constitutional law at the time. Now it may be clearer, why they should have.

[35] Michael Forster, *German Philosophy of Language* (Oxford, UK: Oxford University Press, 2011)

[36] Elad Hakim, "Why Adam Schiff Is Too Biased to Manage Trump's Impeachment Trial," *The Federalist* (January 17, 2020).

https://thefederalist.com/2020/01/17/why-adam-schiff-is-too-biased-to-manage-trumps-impeachment-trial/

undisclosed and even camouflaged behind professors' university credentials and the imprimatur of serious research. In the Ginsburg and Tribe cases, they are aligned with a larger radical ideology concerning Constitutional reform. In the case of Ginsburg, he is actually making a case for not just a "normalization" of casual at-will impeachment action, as I stated, but thereby the implicit dismantling of the constitution itself.[37]

Moreover, under certain conditions, the filtering of facts and perspective stemming from partisan or special-interest motivations, can produce an effective *culpable negligence of omission* standard in law. *Both understanding (rational) and explanatory (causal) factors, are thereby diminished, misunderstood, or especially, deliberately misdirected in social or specifically legal contexts. This shares some relation with theories in cognitive psychology concerning cortex conditioning, resulting in self-audit or inhibition routines that can completely disturb not only rational thought, but instinctive responses centered in active critical processing, and lowering resistance to signal or message bias.*[38] This is in my view also a strictly *moral law and public trust problem* in the professional duty of care in law, and in teaching, perhaps as well when activist proselytizing is distributed in widely disseminated public media

I am not suggesting, to paraphrase Nagel,[39] that "political challenges to legally prescribed meanings" are somehow *per se* inappropriate or inherently mendacious. *My argument has nothing to do with academic freedom, with free speech or with free thought, but more rather with standards of teaching; standards of scholarship, research and writing; with compliance concerning professional legal guidelines; and with quality of university administrative leadership.*[40]

The problem however, has two dimensions. At one level, the political interests pursued by law professors have a corrupting effect on the

---

[37] Cf. "Lawrence Lessig Ponders the Role of a Constitutional Convention (Video)," *Harvard Law Today* (October 5, 2011).

https://today.law.harvard.edu/lessig-ponders-the-role-of-a-constitutional-convention-video/

[38] This embraces a voluminous literature. See: Preston King, *Trusting in Reason: Martin Hollis and the Philosophy of Social Action* (London: Frank Cass, 2003); Michael Barnwell, *The Problem of Negligent Omissions: Medieval Action Theories to the Rescue* (Leiden, Netherlands: Brill, 2010).

[39] Nagel, *The Implosion of American Federalism*, 174, 177.

[40] Nor is it a recommendation for a "moral relativism tending toward nihilism, a pragmatism tending toward an amoral instrumentalism, a realism tending toward cynicism, an individualism tending toward atomism, and a faith in reason and democracy tending toward mere credulity and idolatry."

Roger C. Cramton, "The Ordinary Religion of the Law School Classroom," *Legal Education* 29, no. 3 (1978): 247–263, 262.

internal integrity of university teaching, knowledge and research. At another level, less obvious but more troubling, it plays into the hands of external special interests which draw the university deeper into conflicts of interest and (perhaps intentionally) into becoming an effective vehicle of a multi-institutional strategy involving larger federal, commercial and occasionally foreign organizational networks whereby the university can be instrumentalized as a credentialing, discrediting, or propagandizing entity.

These two levels affect students in turn, both by providing poor examples of reasoning in the former case, and by distracting them away from the pursuit of quality data and knowledge in the latter; that is, the student is left with the false and trivial impression that highly partisan political events are meaningful subjects of justice deliberation. *Student socialization and cognitive maturity are thus trivialized or stunted.* This is why among other reasons, the university is, under ideal conditions, utterly independent.[41]

Embedded within the cycle of the impeachment hearing and trial, however, was perhaps the *sine qua non* of the entire administrative distraction: the simultaneous announcement by the Executive Office, of a Middle East "Deal of the Century," between Israel and Palestine, but negotiated by the U.S. White House and Israel PM Benjamin Netanyahu, with no Palestinian participation.[42] Neo-Bolshevism also provides a coherent framework for reconciling the seemingly diametrically opposite Progressive Left with the neoconservative or "Neo-Con" network. There is in fact nothing "conservative" about neo-conservatism or neo-cons: it is an effective

---

[41] It is also fascinating to consider the very critical distinction between a law professor like Tribe, Ginsburg, Krotoszynski or Bowman, for example, making public statements, recommendations, interpretations, op-ed public relations communications, or being hired as consultants, versus the actual legal representation made by the president's lawyers, for example, who are acting in the role of a lawyer subject to ARDC rules and generating actual institutional legal documents in a formal adjudication. Interestingly, the president's lead counsel, Pat Cipollone, is a law graduate of the University of Chicago and obviously cut from a different cultural cloth. One might wonder if he will be invited back to campus as a guest speaker? Indeed, what percent of the Chicago Law professorship is so professionally represented? Otherwise, my point is that law professors hiding behind their university and their tenure privilege, as opposed to working lawyers exposed to actual legal sanction, are two different realities—one merely casual but pedagogically predatory; the other formal and professionally accountable.

[42] Isahaan Tharoor, "Trump's Deal of the Century Is No Deal t All," *Washington Post* (January 28, 2020).

https://www.washingtonpost.com/world/2020/01/28/trumps-deal-century-is-no-deal-all/

authoritarianism dedicated to military adventurism and defense industry export promotion—an authoritarianism that is central to Israeli geopolitical ambition. Both ideologies are conjoint at their extremist or radical points.[43]

THE PRESIDENTIAL EXECUTIVE ORDER ON COMBATING ANTI-SEMITISM

> *I would like to add something that's not essential to the science, but something I believe, which is that you should not fool the laymen when you're talking as a scientist. I'm talking about a specific, extra type of integrity that is not lying, but bending over backwards to show how you're maybe wrong, [an integrity] that you ought to have when acting as a scientist. And this is our responsibility as scientists, certainly to other scientists, and I think to laymen.*
> Richard Feynman[44]

In the case of President Trump's December 11 Executive Order, University of Chicago Law professor, and Harvard visiting professor, Daniel Hemel published an immediate and carefully timed *New York Times* op-ed,[45] on the heels of White House advisor Jared Kushner's op-ed, *seeking to interpret the EO in legal terms favorable to his ethnic and racial solidarity and interests.*[46] On one hand, that is his right: Hemel's article may be quite understandable, even unremarkable. However, unlike actual judicial procedure and rules, it seeks to falsely claim intent and future or undefined

---

[43] See the excellent *Patterns of Anti-Democratic Thought*, David Spitz (New York: The Macmillan Company, 1949); see also this review:

F.M. Watkins, Untitled review of "*Patterns of Anti-Democratic Thought: An Analysis and a Criticism, with Special Reference to the American Political Mind in Recent Times* by David Spitz; *The Political Theory of Bolshevism: A Critical Analysis* by Hans Kelsen," *Canadian Journal of Economics and Political Science* 16, no. 1(1950): 119–121.

https://www.jstor.org/stable/137637?seq=1

[44] Richard Feynman, "Cargo Cult Science: Some Remarks on Science, Pseudoscience, and Learning How to Not Fool Yourself," Commencement Address at the California Institute of Technology (1974).

http://calteches.library.caltech.edu/51/2/CargoCult.pdf

[45] Daniel Hemel, "Trump's Executive Order Has Firm Legal Grounding," *New York Times* (December 12, 2019).

https://www.nytimes.com/2019/12/12/opinion/trumps-executive-order-has-firm-legal-grounding.html

[46] Jared Kushner, "President Trump Is Defending Jewish Students," *New York Times* (December 11, 2019).

https://www.nytimes.com/2019/12/11/opinion/jared-kushner-trump-anti-semitism.html

harm as a basis of sanction. But are such academic special interest interpretations appropriate in the context of university teaching among young
adults in captive degree programs?

As academic law professors are fond of saying, let's "unpack" his
thinking.

Hemel bases his argument on the assertion that, in his words, "Jews
aren't a race. But anti-Semitism can be racism for legal purposes."

Let's think about that statement.

There are many arguments for and against racial categories, and I
won't rehearse them here. The point is that Mr. Hemel asserts one categorization ("not a race") to serve one objective — *racial immunity for his group*
(—while asserting another category ("but they can be for legal purposes")
to serve another — *racial privilege for his group*.

By "racial immunity" I mean a deflection of criticism over group solidarity and exclusion behavior that is centered in race, racial heritage, and
racial custom. By "racial privilege" I mean an opportunistic application
not just to conform with legal codes addressing anti-discrimination, but a
carve-out of special treatment based on harm and victimization purported to ensue from invoking issues unrelated to that race, strictly in the
political domain, and for political purposes.

Mr. Hemel wants to play it both ways, but the core issue — criticism of
Israel which must be subject to criticism as any other country — he leaves
constructively unaddressed, except to diplomatically recognize that its
aggression toward Palestine (which he merely calls "arguments of those
types" which is a coy way of sanctioning such behavior). He defers to
public sentiment and rather states that such aggression should indeed be
"condemned" verbally, but then quickly blunts the issue by invoking a
blinding comparison *through the moral equivalency fallacy*, by invoking
"Nazi genocide" while signaling several traditional "sympathy" symbols
for bias shielding, including 'Ku Klux Klan,' 'swastikas' and 'vandalized
synagogues').

At this point it gets difficult to discern his argument. In fact, what
group of any identity is discriminated against any longer? Palestinians,
perhaps?[47] That is why it is vital to promote synagogue vandalism, racial
graffiti, or even isolated violence as it is more difficult to tell what precisely his *legal* argument is, because he merely makes a logical error of

---

[47] Ben Jamal, "The Right to Protest against Israel's Policies Threatened," *Signs of the
Times* (January 24, 2020).

https://www.sott.net/article/428035-The-right-to-protest-against-Israels-policies-
threatened

assertion, and then quickly pivots to a history lesson on World War Two to sustain it. But there is another fundamental issue: what *actual discrimination* does a person of Jewish religion, affiliation or heritage, *actually face? Indeed, what actual discrimination does any non-White group face, in any American institution, let alone in higher education?* The answer is, none. That is why it is vital to promote occurrences of synagogue vandalism, racial graffiti, or even isolated violence as a "crisis" that invokes, and immediately subsumes, all the old symbols from World War II. *Victimization must be created, discrimination purported, and intentional harm inferred.* Yet Mr. Hemel surely knows that in law, such an argument would have no currency in a judicial setting, and in civil rights law, actual discriminatory acts must be present, provable and consistently unresolved.

But that isn't what this whole issue is even really about. It's somewhat a straw man, or red herring.

As Jared Kushner stated, "finally, anti-Zionism equals anti-Semitism."[48] But what does this mean? It means that raising factual, observable, verifiable or even debatable observations of Israeli behavior, including especially the economically focused Boycott, Divestment and Sanctions (BDS) initiative, is culturally unacceptable and that unacceptability finds its relief by synthetically embedding it in civil rights protection applying to individuals in higher education environments.

It makes Israel the country into Israel the person.

Yet Hemel argues that such a "person" can be neither a race nor a nationality, *unless it is.* Evidently in his view, Israel and Israelis are an identity. Moreover, penalties for criticism of Israel or of BDS sanctions, if deemed personally injurious in some fashion, would apply quite differently to citizens of the state of Israel. That is, they would not apply, because they cannot extend to foreign jurisdiction; yet the EO makes all persons of Jewish identity, effective Israeli foreign citizens (even without dual citizenship). How does U.S. civil rights law extend to rights of foreign citizens (versus *to* foreign citizens)? Do Israeli laws apply to U.S. citizens when outside Israel? My point is this: if the EO makes a person into a country, then a U.S. law or Directive, can only apply protections or

---

[48] The Trump administration announced it will reveal a Middle East "deal of the century," based on a plan devised by Trump's Orthodox Jewish son-in-law, Jared Kushner. It is a fascinating example of special-interest corruption.

Amir Tibon and Noa Landau, "Trump's Deal of the Century Was Written So the Palestinians Would Reject It," *Haaretz* (January 26, 2020).

https://www.haaretz.com/israel-news/.premium-trump-s-deal-of-the-century-was-written-so-the-palestinians-would-reject-it-1.8443677 assert a "harm" doctrine, within its own country and to its own people. A criticism of the state of Israel, or especially any of its political parties, leaders or corporations, cannot *ipso facto* create harm to an individual, and certainly not in substantive law to a foreigner. If Israel and individuals are equated, then the EO has no appropriate jurisdiction.[49]

If a valid argument, then how can the U.S. federal government financially sanction U.S. institutions of higher learning for discriminating against foreign citizens, or against individuals claiming an identity with a foreign state? The U.S. Constitution does indeed provide certain protections to foreign citizens when in U.S. territory, but by this new rule, the state of Israel would have to be present on U.S. campuses in order for it to be subject to "personhood" and Title VI protection. So—either Israel is a U.S. territory, or, people identifying as "Jewish" would have to either hold exclusive Israeli citizenship, or be *per se* established by treaty as a "state." Since neither of these scenarios are coherent, the argument that "anti-Zionism = anti-Semitism" appears at least factually, indefensible.

But the other identity that would have to be present and defendable, involves equating not merely persons, states and corporations, *but fallaciously equating criticism itself, with actual discrimination*. How can that be tested and proved? Moreover, concerning BDS proper, the state and executive right or assertion of economic sanction, is drawn from specific law.[50] *Moreover, the specific purpose of economic sanction is to force compliance with international law.* The fundamental basis of BDS is its complaint in human rights law. In both movement and defense concerning BDS, there are ethical components, but that is separate from ones in law, in the pursuit of law. Evidently Mr. Hemel's effective position is that Israel is *above the law*, yet the U.S. is not, and its jurisdiction extended to the interpretative treatment of a foreign entity as a person on U.S. soil. This only serves to clarify the inherent incoherency of the entire December EO, and the tortured interpretation made by Mr. Hemel, who also asks the U.S. to break, ignore and suspend *its own constitutional laws* in order to serve his agenda. *There is a fascinating complexity however* in the fact that "BDS" is not a U.S. state sanction, *but a private political public relations initiative*. How

---

[49] See: "What Is an Executive Order?," American Bar Association (November 27, 2018).

https://www.americanbar.org/groups/public_education/publications/teaching-legal-docs/what-is-an-executive-order-/

[50] See J. Curtis Henderson, "Legality of Economic Sanctions Under International Law: The Case Of Nicaragua," *Washington and Lee Law Review* 43 (1986): 167–196.

https://scholarlycommons.law.wlu.edu/wlulr/vol43/iss1/9

does the U.S. apply Title VI against private individuals expressing private opinion concerning other private individuals organizing private voluntary trading or investment restraint against a foreign sovereign nation?

But who or what is suffering "discrimination?" And if so, on what basis, and in what form, exactly? If the discriminatory act is claimed personally injurious, *how can a state suffer personal injury?* If I criticized the Catholic Church (versus the Catholic faith even), I may insult Catholics, but do I discriminate against them? If such a relationship between church and church member were derived from religious identify and religious discrimination, *then Jewish students would have to assert that Israel is a "faith" or a religious entity;* that it is a theocracy (like Iran), or assert that they are members of that faith. *This would mean Catholics could not condemn their Catholic Church (or Vatican City) for sexual predation and criminal law violation due to its discriminatory injury upon persons practicing the Catholic faith on a university campus.* Moreover, it would mean that the vast majority of university faculty aligned with the far Left, and explicitly critical of U.S. government policy, would be likewise discriminating against student conservatives because there is an identity among themselves and the current U.S. government, and therefore the U.S. government should withhold university funding for violating Civil Rights law protecting Conservatives as a race. *Except they're not a race, unless they happen to be (as "White Supremacists").*

But Mr. Hemel also fundamentally confuses and obfuscates the entire matter by focusing on race, and its firm legal grounding in Title VI, *versus the real issue* which is equating Israel as a racial entity, which it cannot *ipso facto* be.

THE NARRATIVE CALCULUS

Criticizing Israel is discriminating against a Jew as an exemplar of the Jewish race because Israel is a racial entity, and *I am Israel*; or Israel is a nationality that I am a member of and therefore of its nationality, and criticism is the same as discrimination *where discrimination is re-defined to be synonymous with perceived personal harm*, where personal harm can be asserted by *predicting* genocidal risk through the invocation of statically anomalous historical events, and by dramatizing or creating current ones; moreover other private individuals complaining about human rights violations by Israel through private lobbying in pursuit of compliance with human rights law, are also engaging in discrimination against me personally, such that U.S. Civil Rights law, shielding discrimination acts based on race, can be enforced through financial *sanction* against a U.S. not-for-profit institution regulated by the U.S. Department of Education, on the basis of the university's role as a *fiduciary agent* of its student body. *That is, U.S. universities are under a new federal contractual obligation to extend speech suppression actively in violation of Constitutional law, on behalf of a foreign entity that is asserting privilege as a person on U.S. soil, or on behalf of selectively identified racial entities [Jews] that selectively equate their race with a foreign state.*

But there's more. How is a state and a person even comingled in the first place, except emotionally, or through nationality? Which means that a Jewish individual is either a racial entity and/or a national one, and is thereby privileged by Title VI, *for actual discriminatory acts*, at the individual level. *For example, is the University of Chicago responsible for Title VI complaints brought by Chinese students asserting discrimination through U.S.-China sovereign economic sanctions?* Is the University an agent of U.S. foreign policy? Does the Hatch Act thereby apply?[51]

Conversely, if the U.S. sanctions Muslim Middle East countries by a travel ban, is the university subject to Title VI discrimination claims by its current Muslim students? Indeed, is the entire Global War on Terror a Title VI cause? By its umbrella influence on U.S. State Department operations, a recent group of Iranian college students were denied entry into the U.S. and immediately forced to return; most were banned for 5 years. They had been currently enrolled on student visas in U.S. universities, had their degree plans interrupted and incurred financial losses in the tens of thousands of dollars. How does this compare in "discrimination" criteria, versus Civil Rights protection for Jewish students asserting discrimination (and injury) based on mere criticism of Israel?[52] If a private

---

[51] It may be provocative to consider if by such law, academic political activism which law professors are effectively defined by federal charter as employees (e.g., a law professor who is also a judge), or agent, such that the Hatch Act is applicable. Indeed, the White House December 11, 2019 EO tying political compliance in Title VI application subject to funding determination, recasts entirely the nature of the university (public and private) and the nature of its employees. This is constructively reinforced when law professors serve on federal investigatory panels (e.g., Sweet, "Stone's Experience on Intelligence Panel: Chicago Sun Times"), act as consultants to government interests, work as judges, are paid with federal funds to advise election candidates or their interests, among other acts that transform their identity (see, e.g., Goldstein, "Teacher to Lose Job under Hatch Act."

[52] "Since August, at least 16 Iranian students have been turned away at airports, losing their chances to study at prestigious universities, amid new tensions between the U.S. and Iran." See Caleb Hampton and Caitlin Dickerson, "'Demeaned and Humiliated': What Happened to These Iranians at U.S. Airports," *New York Times* (January 25, 2020).

group organizes a private boycott of Chinese goods based on Chinese human rights complaint, are Chinese students able to assert personal discrimination under U.S. public law for private acts directed at a foreign state? The answer is yes, actually, *if* such acts led to an extension into personal threat and harm. *But that is a separate body of law* (harassment, stalking, certain torts and related relief for example) *that has nothing to do with Title VI*, or with federal funding conditions. It is removed from effective federal executive control in the courts, and subject to organized standards of adjudication including evidence and appeal, among others.

Moreover, Mr. Hemel also surely knows that sovereignty is not personhood, nor is a political party such as Likud. *A country's political party is a corporation.*[53] If I criticize Google for privacy invasion, or Boeing for airplane design flaws or even the U.S. government for unauthorized war, am I criticizing their employees or leaders directly? Is Boeing suffering discrimination. Is Google a victim? Is the U.S. Government subject to civil rights protection? Mr. Hemel is effectively borrowing a corporate law litigation technique known as "piercing the corporate veil," for a selective ethno-religious argument, *but in pursuit of immunity*. That is, he is voluntarily recasting the company (Israel) into a person (anyone asserting harm) with rights based in universal discrimination. But how does one

---

https://www.nytimes.com/2020/01/25/us/iran-students-deported-border.html

[53] This is debated anecdotally of course, but in civil law it is rather stable. In economics, however, it creates some confusion (see, e.g., Paul Krugman, "A Company Is Not a Country," *Harvard Business Review* (January–February, 1996).

https://hbr.org/1996/01/a-country-is-not-a-company

In a business context, see Sharon Poczter, "Is Running a Country Like Running a Company? Should It Matter?," *Forbes* (July 23, 2012).

https://www.forbes.com/sites/realspin/2012/07/23/is-running-a-country-like-running-a-company-should-it-matter/#15d2043f4865

Interestingly, corporations are domiciled in their Articles and given "national" or state status. In fact, the U.S., for example, *is a private law corporation*. See the plain but direct explanation by David Passieri, "Federal Government: The US Is a Corporation, Not a Country," *Missoulian* (October 11, 2015).

https://missoulian.com/news/opinion/mailbag/federal-government-us-is-a-corporation-not-a-country/article_59915a88-4ca4-5516-853d-caf1f81672f2.html

Commercial corporations also "incorporate" in countries with specific bylaws, statutes, codes, articles, constitutions, and treaties among other features. Moreover, commercial and other corporations, along with individuals, can sue or bring complaints in law against countries—as corporate entities, not as persons. This is otherwise not to be confused with U.S. Code 3002. See "28 U.S. Code § 3002. Definitions."

https://www.law.cornell.edu/uscode/text/28/3002

As for Israel, its founding basis is quite clear: The Israel Corporation, as an example, is incorporated in Israel, and 50% is owned by the Government of Israel.

discriminate, in civil rights, against a country (unless by invading it and suppressing such rights)? According to his logic, and the language of the EO, merely by questioning or criticizing it, but especially by economic discrimination through recommending sanctions (BDS has no actual sanction authority; *but it wields a more dangerous weapon*: knowledge, and human rights accountability).

Mr. Hemel skirts around these difficulties by invoking history, and emotionalism, *and falsely conflating open discourse with oppression and harm,* while holding out the Nazi party as the relevant standard of unacceptable behavior (this is not only illogical but arguably a symptom of psychological difficulty. It emanates from a culturally routinized reinforced memory of Adolf Hitler and the Holocaust, *as weapons to stigmatize* any opposition by criticism, argument, scholarship, or even mere questioning or debate, *that may disturb ideological or political solidarity and its equilibrium in consensus, including especially, in policy and public and private law).*[54] One could arguably invoke a moral law, or natural law argument over not just this particular issue, but all issues relating to prejudice and discrimination—but Hemel doesn't bother to make that argument. Such an argument would be more credible and certainly more honest.[55]

---

[54] The practice of stigmatization language often makes up the overall fabric of legal and policy arguments, and extends into very broad but common pubic symbols that provoke emotional, sentimental, sympathetic, or agitated response, and thereby move in like a fog over the abuses or flaws in reason that are often necessary to advance special-interest positions. A recent op-ed by Jonathan A. Greenblatt, Chief Executive Officer of the Anti-Defamation League, is an excellent example, which also adds to its "deflection and dissimulation arsenal" a new ideological agenda based in what might call fear of "White Terror."

https://www.usatoday.com/story/opinion/2020/01/26/auschwitz-liberation-ban-holocaust-denial-on-facebook-column/4555483002/

[55] Nor does he make even one argument in a Western philosophical tradition; for example, Kant's *categorical imperative.*

Kant holds that, for all of which we are capable based on autonomy and autocracy, we cannot know with certainty that any finite rational being has ever acted in a way that displays true or genuine moral worth—that is, non-egoistically. Otherwise put, for all that we know based on the conception of moral agency at the heart of Kant's ethics, it is possible that all finite rational agents capable of morality and virtue demonstrate nothing beyond heteronomy of will, acting only from motives of self-interest and its principle of (personal) happiness.

Robert Hanna, "Why the Better Angels of Our Nature Must Hate the State," *International Journal of Philosophy* No. 6 (December 2017).

https://www.con-textoskantianos.net/index.php/revista/article/view/281/345

What he cannot invoke is common or civil law; a general legal theory argument; or even a logically reasoned one. *His argument is legalistic deception, which can only survive by a willing suspension of disbelief, attended by linguistic reformulation, and reality thereby altered or even transformed.* Mr. Hemel not only actively adulterates strictly *legal* reasoning, but at a deeper level, acts from "incompletely reasoned contemporary liberal theories of rights, which rarely discuss those additional ontological, epistemological and psychological foundations on which the defense of liberal individualistic rights ultimately rests.[56]

Beneath these more visible dissimulations exists however, another important one which explains Mr. Hemel's advocacy for his larger special-interest network.[57]

He declares, in his words, that "Jews aren't a race. But anti-Semitism can be racism for legal purposes." Why would he take this particular position? Is he obligated to explain his assumptions? Why not discuss why he feels they should be otherwise be so categorized? Many if not all countries — except strictly *Western* ones including the U.S., Canada, New Zealand, Australia and the UK — define themselves racially. China for Chinese. Japan for the Japanese. Korea for Koreans. India for Indians. Mongolia for Mongols. Why not Israel for Jews?[58]

Why is Hemel careful to conform to the narrative that Jews are not a race, or even a nationality, except in his argument, instead *selectively and opportunistically categorized in order to invoke the parameters of U.S. civil rights law and conflated with a foreign national identity*?

There are two primary reasons.

One, declaring Jews a race, or a nationality even, brings into focus *a distinction that uncloaks* their social integration and institutional embeddedness *in Western countries.* The U.S. in particular, is vital to the establishment, procurement and expansion of the state of Israel. This is realized

---

[56] Gunnar Beck, *Fichte and Kant on Freedom, Rights, and Law* (Lanham, MD: Lexington Books, 2008)

[57] An element of Hemel's strictly legal dissimulation concerns his use of the word 'grounded'. He claims that such racial categorization is grounded in law. But that is incorrect, or at least, not proven by him. He substitutes a selective patchwork of U.S. history, adds some anecdote, symbolism and innuendo, and advances this narrative as law. He would be better served by being more honest and discussing race and nationalism within its global context, but there is a reason he does not, as I describe above.

[58] That of course is precisely how Israel forms and conducts its internal domestic affairs, especially under Benjamin Netanyahu and the Likud party. Indeed, Netanyahu's orchestrated "diaspora repatriation" programs (for example in France) are targeted specifically at Jewish, and only Jewish, individuals.

not only financially, but culturally, socially and especially, politically in foreign policy (and in warfare). Two, the ability of Jews to consolidate critical roles in U.S. society necessary to steer interests generally favorable to Israel (in business, media, government, banking, law and higher education for example) requires cultural integration, without which Israeli interests would be considered de-linked from U.S. ones.

ABSTRACTION AND PERMEATION OF THE NARRATIVE

The importance of cultural integration extends to "mirroring" the "Judeo-Christian" narrative—i.e., adopting the external signs of assimilation (e.g., no foreign accents or separate communities). While Jews are portrayed as typical Americans, other groups are not, e.g., the Muslim "terror" narrative and the Arab/Muslim "otherness" doctrine, among others. Cultural integration also requires an explicit technological and information bi-lateral exclusivity (often abused by Israel through re-selling, especially to China[59]). All these elements and others, demand not distinction or otherness, *but sameness* (but Hemel's argument exactly articulates why a dual-identity is politically necessary). Racial and national legal distinctions threaten integration—except through careful appropriation of U.S. law which is readily fungible, co-opted and rationalized (hence Hemel's public media essay disseminated in the NYT). This project is protected by promoting (or creating) sensational aggression (e.g., damage to synagogues, lone-shooter home invasions, and reference to swastikas, skin-heads, or even Nazi history). Indeed, the constant invocation of "Nazism" is absolutely vital to sustaining the special-interest narrative, and especially an insistence (and in Germany a criminal law enforcement) on the precise number of casualties, because otherwise World War II and the holocaust, *are statistical anomalies*. So for social science researchers, this

---

[59] Danit Gal, "The U.S.-Israel Technology Triangle," Council on Foreign Relations (July 19, 2019).

https://www.cfr.org/blog/us-china-israel-technology-triangle

Duncan Clarke, "Israel's Unauthorized Arms Transfers," *Foreign Policy* No. 99 (Summer, 1995): 89–109.

The symbiosis among Israel and China is increasingly being uncovered, as a recent arrest at Harvard University reveals a multi-million dollar science and technology transfer scheme orchestrated by Harvard's Chairman of the Chemistry Department, Charles M. Lieber, who is pictured in the NYT article announcing his arrest, at a black-tie "award" event in Jerusalem, Israel.

Ellen Barry, "U.S. Accuses Harvard Scientist of Concealing Chinese Funding," *New York Times* (January 28, 2020).

https://www.nytimes.com/2020/01/28/us/charles-lieber-harvard.html

presents a conundrum: if you normalize the data, the period 1940–1945 is not anomalous for Jews, and *within the larger casualty set*, their experience is a small sub-set. This is why the data must be constantly re-characterized in narrative terms, and linked to equal if not greater statistical anomaly in current affairs.[60] The saying "never again" is inaccurate from a motivational perspective. It is rather "forever." Forever stylized, communicated, narrated, distributed, and embedded in special-interest routines leading in many cases to legal carve-outs such at the December 2019 EO.

In this regard, distinction can be accepted and understood by the public, while its "otherness" can be switched off in larger institutional settings *dependent on cultural mirroring*. Interestingly, the otherness concept is deflected by systematic political support for Left ideology including mass immigration (in the U.S. and Europe through the creation of a roaming war refugee class from the Middle East that has destabilized much of Western Europe). This dilutes or destabilizes White political and cultural dominance, while simultaneously reinforcing Jewish and Israeli consolidation. Such consolidation or at least promotion and reinforcement, also requires effective ideological recruitment, and its subsumption into normalized economic channels such as law. Indeed, the legal system and the law school are the vital "training camps" of a variety of special-interest interpretations, all cemented by unified progressive identitarianism. In this regard, President Trump is merely (like all U.S. presidents) an opportunity for influence and manipulation, and if one merely surveys the current administration's policies, they perfectly fit the larger positions Mr. Hemel represents.

But let's say I'm wrong about all this—that openly criticizing the actions of one state versus another, or among others, is indeed inherently personally injurious, discriminatory, and creates a victim. How could I move such an argument in a court of law? How can personal hate language be constitutionally protected, but language critical of an impersonal entity is not?

---

[60] For example, in media hysteria over the recent Virginia Second Amendment rally, where the Governor was pressured to enact a state of emergency, linked to "White Nationalism" and violence. No such thing occurred, and even sympathetic media was forced to admit the utterly civil, peaceful, and professional assembly of Virginia's open-carry citizens.

Dan Gainor, "Virginia Gun Rights Rally Incredibly Peaceful, Defying Expectations of Hysterical Media," Fox News (January 21, 2020).

https://www.foxnews.com/opinion/virginia-gun-rights-rally-peaceful-media-dan-gainor

THE COLLISION OF FREE SPEECH DOCTRINE AND SPECIAL INTEREST RADI-CALISM

Although science is capable of linear advancement, the same is not true of law, where the same insights and mistakes tend to recur again and again.
Richard A. Epstein, *How Progressives Rewrote the Constitution*[61]

This brings us to Mr. Hemel's other glaring legal infirmity: *free speech doctrine.* He seeks to activate a preemptive, or pro forma suppression, of speech (even thoughts) critical of the state of Israel. He solves for this infirmity in part by using modern identitarianism as an emotional and cognitive aid for speech suppression, and the acceptance of speech suppression on identitarian grounds. Which is what the December 11 EO is inherently serving. In this regard alone, the presidential EO has no *per se* legal grounding, which is why the campus initiative was activated strictly by executive order — it took careful internal maneuvering of the executive office and a bypassing of courts, congress, states and private law. But this raises another thorny legal problem that Hemel ignores as well. *The normalization of executive order privilege followed the ratification of the U.S. Patriot Act.* This act stands poised over the constitution, ready to be activated at-will, over any judgment deemed in the "national interest," including even suspicions of thought deviation posed by such threats. And it authorizes the use of force, confinement or other measures to achieve these ends.

Fascinatingly, it was through EO assertions that the same White House was able to issue a blanket stop-order against people from "Muslim" nations who are considered unacceptable risks, this preventing them from entering the U.S. *How can an order of exclusion be based on racial, ethnic or national bases (Muslim) but another order provide an effective 'writ of habeas corpus' to others asserting unlawful psychological or emotional "confinement" for the same reasons, and even providing relief in U.S. civil rights laws?*

This is the awesome power of the new ideological "iron square" on America's college campuses consisting of identity, terror, security and climate, and specifically defined on racial and religious grounds. Mr. Hemel draws his inspiration and his insulation directly from it, while advancing the false construct of selective sovereign immunity based on a selective racial identity. Catching someone in logical fallacy and other cognitive errors is simple. Where is the actual "harm" located? In the classroom — and the discrimination and victimization, measured in the cognitive arrest of captive university students.

---

[61] Richard A. Epstein, *How Progressives Rewrote the Constitution* (Washington, DC: The Cato Institute, 2006), vii.

The Occidental Quarterly, vol. 20, no. 2, Summer 2020

I have paused *and wondered if I'm missing something in Hemel's motivations*; perhaps a more subtle or sophisticated or elegant explanation as to what basis he and others that make similar appeals but defy a recognizable anchor in law or logic, may be arguing from. Perhaps a natural law assumption; or a moral non-natural one (in, for example, G.E. Moore's *Principia Ethica*), or perhaps a self-evident argument, from a "Finnis reconstruction.[62]" But this would be resting essentially on practical reason, and on that basis, his argument, and others like it, find a hard time making their case when there is such an abundance of sound, even mass opposition (e.g., the National Students for Justice in Palestine[63]). One might point to Hart's concept of natural necessities (and per Hobbs); that is, *a "survival" calculus that is believed superior to law.* Maybe even a form of "neo-scholastic" perspective.

However, to achieve that, much is forsaken. Hillary Putnam's exploration in "The Fact/Value Dichotomy" I think is instructive in its "rejection of the idea that while factual claims can be rationally established or refuted, claims about value are wholly subjective, and not capable of being rationally argued for or against." This may be a core problem with Hemel's unacknowledged or undisclosed assumptions.[64] *Ultimately, I think he may represent a radicalized form of legal positivism* (perhaps a 'hijacked' form is more accurate) that Putnam smartly rejects in his separation of facts and values. He and special-interest advocates like him may assert rather a traditional Utilitarianism, but their actual abandonment of normative equity (i.e., equal treatment as a norm, as opposed to normative appropriation) undermines such an assertion.[65]

---

[62] Kevin Paul Lee, "The Conceptions of Self-Evidence in the Finnis Reconstruction of Natural Law," unpublished ms: Raleigh, NC: Campbell Law School (February 11, 2019).
   http://dx.doi.org/10.2139/ssrn.3332340

[63] See "SJP Condemns Trump's Executive Order," *National Students for Justice in Palestine* (n/d).
   https://www.nationalsjp.org/sjpunitedstatement.html

[64] See Alexei Angelides, "The Last Collapse?" for some basic background on a version of "radicalism of legal positivist" (versus my *radicalization* argument).
   Alexei Angelides, "The Last Collapse?," *Philosophy of Science* 71, no. 3 (2004): 402–411.
   https://www.jstor.org/stable/10.1086/421540?seq=1
   See also Brian Leiter, "The Radicalism of Legal Positivism," University of Chicago Public Law and Legal Theory Working Paper No. 303 (2010).
   https://chicagounbound.uchicago.edu/cgi/viewcontent.cgi?article=1334&context=public_law_and_legal_theory

[65] Angelides notes: "Putnam engages his philosophical discussion with contemporary economic theory in order to motivate his central claim: that taking a somewhat interesting distinction between facts and values and inflating it into a dichotomy can, and often

This radical positivism is continually reinforced through shame and victimization routines, combined with authority framing in the institutional hierarchy and media. The result is an effective new "rule of recognition" that has quietly penetrated normal public discourse, resulting in favoritism in the political economy, such as favoritism resulting in a partisan foreign policy.

The current Executive Office Middle East "peace plan" is an example.[66] There may even be a coherent argument directed at such writings as Hemel, Tribe, Ginsburg, and others, that is organized within *avoidable harm* doctrine. In my view, acting in the capacity of a law professor, under the guidelines of the Association of American Law Schools in ways that grossly mislead students, *is not unrelated to a moral and professional restraint from doing harm.*[67]

Are the presidential executive order and the "deal of the century" Middle East plan related? Was it coincidence that an all-consuming impeachment trial was conducted while the Middle East was being carved up without deliberation? Indeed, why was Benjamin Netanyahu at the White House in December 2019 (preceded by Secretary Steven Mnuchin and Jared Kushner in Jerusalem),[68] followed by the activation of speech suppression executive orders, the activation of the "Covid" narrative, and the authoritarian decree of home-quarantine and economic lockdown instructions, the latter administered through coordinated   the various states, combined with a ubiquitous dissemination of a terrorizing virus

---

does, lead to disastrous policy decisions." The EO and its ideological context may be an example in my view of just such disastrous policy

Angelides, "The Last Collapse?," 402.

[66] Nathan Thrall, "Trump's Middle East Peace Plan Exposes the Ugly Truth," *New York Times* (January 29, 2020).

https://www.nytimes.com/2020/01/29/opinion/trump-peace-plan.html.

A "deal" moreover requires at least two parties to the deal: in this case, only the U.S. and Israel were present; Palestinian interests were not even invited to the White House. That makes it not a deal, but a diktat.

[67] "Law Professors in the Discharge of Ethical and Professional Responsibilities," The Association of American Law Schools (November 17, 1989).

https://www.aals.org/about/handbook/good-practices/ethics/

[68] There was also a follow-on "Holocaust Conference" in Jerusalem that was heavily promoted through diplomatic channels. Even Sweden officially attended, after being heavily lobbied by the Simon Wiesenthal Center, followed by a rare Israel state visit by Sweden's Prime Minister.

"SWC to Swedish PM: Cancel International Conference on Anti-Semitism," Simon Wiesenthal Center (November 5, 2019).

http://www.wiesenthal.com/about/news/swc-to-swedish-pm-cancel.html,:

narratology which was carefully crafted and propagated through by the Fourth Estate. Collectively these events are giving Israel cover to systematically carry out its full-spectrum assault on Palestine, effectively engaging in systematic genocide, which depends on a panoply of suppression tools including speech, public assembly, and economic activity?

Last, and of course central to the EO, Hemel, as a law professor at the University of Chicago and Harvard, completely misses the fascinating legal implications to free speech doctrine on university campuses. The University of Chicago newspaper, the *Chicago Maroon*, one of the nation's most iconic student media platforms since 1892, ran a story referring to University president Robert Zimmer, titled, "Zimmer Talks First Amendment, Finance on Davos Panel."[69] In it, Zimmer is quoted, saying "I keep telling people who congratulate me on defending the First Amendment that it's not about the First Amendment .... As a private University we are not subject to the First Amendment."

That's not quite correct.

President Trump's recent Executive Orders were directed specifically at universities and colleges, one Order involving conservative speech accommodation, the other asserting Title VI protection of the Civil Rights Act to broader ethno-religious groups on campus. Both threaten the withholding of federal funding if such Executive Orders are found to be in violation by any member of the university sector. This underscores the inherent long-standing nature and dependency of public finance in the mix of university funding sources. But is goes decades back in history: outside of a handful of for-profit higher education companies, all universities and colleges in the U.S. are tax-exempt and thereby publicly subsidized, as are student loans, guaranteed by the federal government (totaling over $1.5 trillion). Moreover, their entire operating status and degree-granting authority — their "license" to practice — come directly from the U.S. Government's Department of Education accreditation power.[70]

Trump's executive orders alone, by their inherent federal funding conditions, also effectively ratify decades-old U.S. case law concerning constitutional free speech, and other rights, on university campuses, especially in Dickey v. Alabama, (Dickey v. Alabama State Board of Education,

---

[69] Tony Brooks, "Zimmer Talks First Amendment, Finance on Devos Panel," *Chicago Maroon* (January 22, 2020).
https://www.chicagomaroon.com/article/2020/1/22/zimmer-davos/

[70] U. S. Department of Education, "Accreditation: Postsecondary Education Institutions" (n/d; accessed June 15, 2020).
https://www.ed.gov/accreditation

273 F. Supp. 613 M.D. Ala. 1967) whose Constitutional law judgement was centrally determined by "tax-supported colleges or universities." It does not say "tax-financed" but rather broader federal funding receipts that characterize all higher education institutional capital structures. Moreover, any student or university constituent could, if necessary to defend such rights, constructively pierce pretentions to private university status, given the inherent, and growing, government finance roles in the university complex (including military and defense ones, and in Chicago's case, its federally compensated administration of the Fermi and Argonne Labs, both federal Department of Energy and Department of Defense research installations).

There is no longer (if there ever was) a "private" university, and there are no enforceable exemptions to, or survivable defenses against, constitutional law obligations, including free speech rights, in higher education. Zimmer's position is not only tenuous, but constructively wrong. At an institutional level, this makes the dissonance between the university's principles purporting to ratify free speech, and its *ex-ante* threat of discipline enforcement in Statute 21 of the university's Chicago Trustees Restated Articles of Incorporation,[71] specifically against it (under the University's pretension to private interpretation of free speech), an obvious legal infirmity.[72]

---

[71] Cf. Friedrich Nietzsche, in *Daybreak*, 1, 13:

Towards the re-education of the human race. Men of application and goodwill assist in this one work: to take the concept of punishment which has overrun the whole world and root it out! There exists no more noxious weed! Not only has it been implanted into the consequences of our actions—and how dreadful and repugnant to reason even this is, to conceive cause and effect as cause and punishment!—but they have gone further and, through this infamous mode of interpretation *with the aid of the concept of punishment, robbed of its innocence the whole purely chance character of events.* Indeed, they have gone so far in their madness as to demand that we feel our very existence to be a punishment—it is as though the education of the human race had hitherto been directed by the fantasies of jailers and hangmen! (Italics mine.)

[72] There is also a disturbing "leakage" in U.S. public funding, channelled through the University of Chicago, which goes directly to Israel through its molecular engineering program—in part funded by the Pritzker family specifically for Israeli technology development, with no restraints in technology export law based in national security, and carefully characterized as benign technical assistance in water treatment. There are other motivations for this project beyond strictly local academic ones. These include hydration and broader strategic development of the Negev, done in conjunction with the Zuckerberg Institute and Ben Gurion University in a deal signed by Zimmer, Rahm Emanuel

Extending ultimately from these ideological positions from special interests, *is the cost to the rest of us:* unbridled selective geopolitical expansion, influence and social destabilization. Because that is the basis of criticism that Israel is most sensitive to: its territorial expansion *based in ethnic, racial and religious exclusivity,* and perhaps most of all, what makes what would ordinally be two separate events — executive orders and an impeachment — into an identity: the greatest threat and the greatest opportunity is the effective administrative conquering of Russia. That is precisely why "Ukraine" is so central to the impeachment, and why critical suppression and silencing against Israel's growing lethal aggression (direct or through its proxy, the U.S.) by inserting it into U.S. civil rights code tied to financial bribery and sanction, is the tip of the spear in realizing the end-game of the GWOT — the destruction of Iran and the influence of Russia in the Middle East. The December EO is in reality, war-time government censorship. The ultimate question however, may be, who has already been invaded?

---

and former Israeli Prime Minister Shimon Perez; that is, it is also an effective export or technology transfer project that obviously has national security implications (somewhat mitigated politically by the construction of the first U.S. military base in the Negev). Molecular engineering also has inherent, specific applications in new weapons science — it is among the most aggressively pursued science and technology projects by the Pentagon, including polymer and nanoscale technology. It is not likely that any applications, even those that are properly civilian, will otherwise find application in synthetic climate or hydration projects in the larger Middle East desert zones; however molecular engineering can also be used for desertification with application to land conversion and demographic modification for the oil and gas fracking industry. As reported in public media, Zimmer had a "long-simmering interest in creating a joint partnership with an Israeli university." Combined with investments by University Trustee Chairman Joseph Neubauer in Israeli technology and weapons corporations (disclosed in public filings) one could reasonably question the conflicts of interest involved, as well as the implication of Zimmer's remark that this project has "potential applications far beyond local issues.

"Israel-Chicago Partnership Targets Water Resource Innovations," *UChicago News* (June 5, 2013).

https://news.uchicago.edu/story/israel-chicago-partnership-targets-water-resource-innovations

Hydrology also has military and weapons-based applications.

"No Reprieve! Israel Continues Flooding Gaza Farmland to Destroy Palestinian Food Supply," *Middle East Monitor* (January 24, 2020).

https://www.sott.net/article/428033-No-reprieve-Israel-continues-flooding-Gaza-farmland-to-destroy-Palestinian-food-supply

CONCLUSION: IS THERE A DOMINANT THIRD POLITICAL PARTY IN AMERICA?

Palestine is fast disappearing and fulfilling the objectives of Israel's founding fathers. Over many decades, Israel has developed and refined policies to disperse, imprison and impoverish the Palestinian people, in a relentless effort to destroy them as a nation. It has industrialized Palestinian despair through ever more sophisticated systems of curfews, checkpoints, walls, permits and land grabs. Israel has transformed the West Bank and Gaza into laboratories for testing the infrastructure of confinement, creating a lucrative "defense" industry by pioneering the technologies needed for urban warfare, crowd control and collective punishment.

Jonathan Cook, *Disappearing Palestine: Israel's Experiments in Human Despair*[73]

A culture that is at once moralistic, self-righteous, alienated and in a minority will constantly be tempted to break the rules of political discourse — indeed to conduct its struggles in ways that preclude the use of the word "discourse" — and to gain its ends by deception or outright falsehood.

Judge Robert H. Bork, *The Tempting of America: The Political Seduction of the Law*[74]

By adopting a political and legal ideology of social justice that seeks to define and direct cognitive sensing, framing and prioritization, one ipso facto submits to a perceived necessary authority, and is prompted by this authority with repetitive messages, cultural narratives and visual symbols that together seek to form a dominant memetic or psychologically embedded viral unit of information, that is independent and self-replicating. It acts as a "code" on how to feel, what to think, and how to behave. This explains the susceptibility of U.S. political, educational and legal machinery, to guidance, prompting and direction from special-interest cultural authority and its willingness to serve it. Law and law training, then become a metaphysics of involuntary, externally promoted sensory provocation, conditioning, and emotional response, rather than a discipline of internal, self-initiated structured probity, within rational, sovereign deliberation.

V. S. Solovyev

---

[73] Jonathan Cook, *Disappearing Palestine: Israel's Experiments in Human Despair* (London: Zed Books, 2006), 7.

[74] Robert H. Bork, *The Tempting of America: The Political Seduction of the Law* (New York: Simon & Schuster, 2009), 342.

The Occidental Quarterly, vol. 20, no. 2, Summer 2020

In discussing a third party, I refer to a dominant, highly organized, efficient and resource-rich political party coalesced around Israeli interests. Those interests include strictly economic ones (including organized crime); religious and ethnic enthusiasms, and geopolitical ambitions (the pan-Israel construct). Is the Likud party an effective third party in the U.S.?[75] Although criticism of Israel — such as John Mearsheimer and Stephen Walt discuss in *The Israel Lobby and U.S. Foreign Policy*[76] — can be seen in a simple mono-directional manner (i.e., aid and finance flowing from the U.S. to Israel), Israel also serves as an "incubator" for U.S. domestic security policy, law enforcement, and related State projects.

I paint a picture of a complex political network that is intellectually centered in elite law schools that codifies activism and provides a pipeline of ideologues into the government apparatus. It is almost entirely made up of pro-Israel radicals (Henry Kissinger, Laurence Tribe, Louis Kaplow, Cass Sunstein, Bruce Ackerman, Alan Dershowitz, Eric Posner, and others provide a "senior authority" symbolism that is reinforced with dozens of second- and third-tier ideological colleagues, including those in foreign and military policy, and financial institutional and media influence roles such as Max Boot, Dov Zakheim or Peter Orszag). Such ideology is channeled into policy that is then "sold" through the Congressional apparatus and with careful appointee maneuvering in senior advisor and administrative roles in State, the White House, the Pentagon and the intelligence, security and law enforcement agencies. The model rests largely on an elitist intellectual identity which is necessary in order to anchor relatively complex conceptual and linguistic framing that can then flow through an elitist social network.

While this picture has been described before,[77] it rarely puts its finger on the more sensitive, if difficult ethno-religious and cultural content that is the inherent basis of the instincts, motivations, interests and ideology that initiate, manage and distribute the necessary intellectual content through the institutional architecture that converts it operationally. The central operational coding consists of a "Neo-Bolshevism" that projects a

---

[75] This is more feasible than may first appear. By Likud, I also mean "Zionist" as it is most aligned with that philosophy. Likud activism and support has several U.S. nodes, but one that is primary is the modern university. This has a tiered character where the most systematic and networked activism is in U.S. "elite" universities, followed by a broader penetration in "R1 Doctoral Universities–Very High Research Activity," and finally in elite colleges, and regional universities.

[76] John Mearsheimer and Stephen Walt, *The Israel Lobby and U.S. Foreign Policy* (New York: Farrar, Straus and Giroux, 2007).

[77] See Thomas Sowell, *Intellectuals and Society*.

social justice and contract philosophy, but is at its core a fascistic, authoritarian ethno-religious neurosis that manifests in systematic institutional social predation, including most recently, the roll-out of long-incubated plans that seek to dismantle several traditional Western cultural traditions and replace them with a de facto theocracy centered in economic and military control, ethnic cleansing and depopulation management, that function under broad environmental activism appeals, and key social controls that isolate and de-socialize public interaction while increasing public economic dependence and cognitive infantilism.

V. S. Solovyev is an alumnus of the University of Chicago.

Schopenhauer and Judeo-Christian Life-Denial

Thomas Dalton

Vitam impendere vero ("Dedicate one's life to truth.")
—Juvenal, *Satire* IV, 91[1]

Every movement needs its icons, the alt-right no less than any other social-political ideology. Any icon—a term deriving from the Greek *eikôn*, meaning a likeness or image—serves to embody key elements or aspects of a particular outlook, or to encapsulate certain key values. Within Christianity, the image of a crucified Jesus serves this purpose, as does an empty cross, which signifies his alleged resurrection. Within the alt-right, we have our own secular heroes, often drawn from among the great philosophers and intellectual figures of Western history, among whom I would include Socrates, Plato, and Aristotle; French thinkers like Rousseau, Diderot, and Voltaire; and leading German intellectuals like Kant, Goethe, and Nietzsche. All have contributed seminal and indispensable ideas to the Western project.

But special standing is reserved for Arthur Schopenhauer (1788–1860), a man of exceptional insight and courage. At once a brilliant metaphysician and a visionary social critic, Schopenhauer combined both aspects of his persona in his two main works, *The World as Will and Representation* (1818)[2] and *Parerga and Paralipomena* (1851)[3]. It is worthwhile examining his views on life and death, Christianity, and the Jews. There are valuable lessons here for us all.

---

[1] This is the opening quotation in Schopenhauer's *Parerga and Paralipomena* (Oxford: Oxford University Press, 1851/1974; E. F. J. Payne, trans.). Original from Juvenal, *circa* 110 AD.

[2] *World as Will and Representation* (New York: Dover, 1969; E. F. J. Payne, trans); hereafter *WWE*. The German title is also rendered in English as *The World as Will and Idea*, owing to the ambiguity of the word *Vorstellung*.

[3] A 'parergon' is a supplement or addition, and a 'paralipomenon' is something omitted or overlooked. Hence this book comprises a number of essays and aphorisms on a variety of topics that are supplemental to Schopenhauer's main work. As an aside, I note that some of Schopenhauer's other "books," such as *Essays and Aphorisms* and *On the Suffering of the World*, are just extracts from *Parerga and Paralipomena*.

METAPHYSICS OF THE WILL

Let's start with the big metaphysical picture. In its broad outline, Schopenhauer's worldview consists of a universe of struggle, strife, and conflict—of tension and opposition which is only ever temporarily relieved, except to resume once more later on, in new and more potent forms. We see this clearly, he said, in the human realm, in the guise of war, oppression, and criminality. We see it in the mundane struggles of daily life, for money, friends, influence, power. We see it in countless minor actions and decisions that we all make, every day, aiming at something new, something better, something more. Every human action, even the most trivial, is a manifestation of a want, a desire, an urging, a striving—in short, of the *will*. As such, all social conflict reduces, ultimately, to a battle of wills.

But this situation is not limited to humans. We see a comparable picture in the animal kingdom, in the struggle for existence, for mates, for food, and for survival. We see it in plants, in their battle for sunlight and water, and for nutrients in the soil. And we see it even in inanimate nature, via such forces as gravitation, magnetism, and electrostatics. All the world, said Schopenhauer, is comprised, in its essence, of struggle, strife, frustration, and opposition; all the world is a manifestation of the will. The metaphysics here are fascinating and strikingly original, but I won't elaborate for now. Here, we are most concerned with the social realm and the far-reaching implications of seeing "the world as will."

For we humans, as mentioned, our daily life is a constant expression of our will. We *want*: want food, want drink, want material goods, want sex, want prestige, want power. Different people express their wills differently, but the essential nature of all people is the same: a constant striving or desiring for something. This has two important consequences. First, since we all are constantly striving—often for the same limited things—we are thereby engaged in an endless competition with others. As in any competition, there are (a few) winners and (many) losers. The losers become frustrated, disappointed, depressed, perhaps angry, perhaps aggressive. They either vow to try harder next time, or they give up altogether. Even the winners—and we all do win, from time to time—are not really satisfied. After a short-lived sense of relief or satisfaction, we immediately settle into a new sense of desiring and wanting. The sweetness of victory is fleeting. Soon we are either fending off jealous rivals, or we are constructing new, higher desires that we hope to fulfill. At best, we are simply bored.

Hence the second consequence: the basic reality of human life is a condition of unsatisfied want, endless craving, relentless competition, and unfulfilled desire—in other words, of *suffering*. Our lot in life is a constant striving for things that we can never really possess, least of all 'happiness,' and therefore the tangible reality of life is pain, suffering, and want. 'Happiness' or 'satisfaction' are merely temporary releases from such pain; therefore, happiness and pleasure are *negative* in their nature, and pain and suffering are the positive realities of the world.

Thus we arrive at Schopenhauer's infamous pessimism. Life is a task, a chore, indeed, a punishment. We are all condemned to lives of greater or lesser suffering, sometimes physical, sometimes psychological, sometimes intense, sometimes mild—but ever-present and always looming greater in the future. The end of this life of suffering comes only with the 'great suffering' of physical death, which we all dread, and which therefore weighs upon our heads as yet more suffering. It would have been better, he concludes, if we had never been born.

What to do? Such a depressing picture almost inclines one to suicide. And yet Schopenhauer masterfully turns the picture around for us, finding a way through the morass of existence. First, he says, we are strangely fortunate that the world is as it is. Were it otherwise—if we somehow attained fulfillment and satisfaction on a regular basis, life would become truly pointless. We would either be driven insane by boredom, or would create artificial conflicts and struggles, wars and mass atrocities, simply to have a reason for being. Failing these, we might simply end our own lives—ironic, that the suicidal person is the one who has all his desires satisfied, not the one, like us, condemned to a life of struggle and pain. Suffering, said Schopenhauer, was like the ballast of a ship; it keeps us on the straight-and-narrow, keeps us focused, and drives us forward. Paradoxically, we ought to be grateful for our condition; if nothing else, it leads us to the ultimate metaphysical truths about the world.

Be that as it may, we still need to live our lives, preferably with a minimum of suffering. Hence we are faced with a profound dilemma: Life is desire, and desire leads to the very suffering that we seek to avoid. On the one hand, then, we ought logically to minimize or reduce ("deny") our desires. But this is tantamount to *denying life*. This may be a theoretical possibility for a saint or a god, but it is an unworkable plan for the real world. At its worst, a 'life of life-denial' is an incoherent and self-annihilating concept, one appropriate only for a pathological individual.[4]

Therefore, to live, we must accept the struggle and pain of life, keep our expectations low, press ahead, and hope for the best. This is the only practical conclusion. Yes, we ought to minimize our desires where possible: avoid a fixation on money, material things, status—all those things that Jews, for example, obsess about, and thus foist upon the public mind as the ultimate goals in life. We should not be too concerned about a nebulous and facile goal like 'happiness,' which in any case is virtually impossible in a world of perpetual strife. We ought not expect that things will necessarily turn out well, and therefore not be disappointed when they don't. Life goes on, the struggle goes on—such it is.

It's a striking moral picture that Schopenhauer paints for us, one that is hard to refute. I think we all can relate to such thinking in our everyday experience. Much of this rings true, and yet we rarely follow the logic out to the full implications.

If it all sounds vaguely Buddhist, that's because it is. One of Schopenhauer's great surprises, and greatest satisfactions, was his discovery of Buddhist philosophy in the 1830s, well after he had written volume one of his monumental work, *World as Will and Representation*. There are many obvious affinities, and Schopenhauer viewed himself as independently coming to the same eternal truths as the Buddha but from an entirely different route, and with a much firmer philosophical foundation. Their prescriptions were essentially the same: end suffering via an elimination of desire and attachment, which is the source of that suffering.[5] But Buddhism was entangled in a mythological schema involving *samsara* or a cycle of endless reincarnation and rebirth, and of *nirvana*, conceived as an end to that cycle. Schopenhauer had no patience for such mythology but he respected the metaphysical insight, and placed it, in his mind, on a superior rational footing.

---

[4] Nietzsche recognized and acknowledged this very point: "For an ascetic, life is a self-contradiction. ... [For such a man,] life somehow turns against itself, denies itself" (*Genealogy of Morals* III, sec. 11). And again: "Morality, as it has so far been understood—as it has in the end been formulated once more by Schopenhauer, as 'negation of the will to live'—is the very instinct of decadence, which makes an imperative of itself. It says: '*Perish!*'" (*Twilight of the Idols* V, sec. 5).

[5] Putting an end to personal desires and attachment to material things was in fact the third of the Buddha's "four noble truths."

"ONE TRUE CHRISTIAN"

But it wasn't only Buddhism that Schopenhauer found affinity with; it was also there, to a surprising degree, in Christianity. In fact, his alignment with 'original' or 'true' Christianity was so strong that Schopenhauer considered himself the 'one true Christian,' and the only such person in all of modern history: "my teaching could be called Christian philosophy proper, paradoxical as this may seem to those who do not go to the root of the matter, but stick merely to the surface".[6] This astonishing conclusion demands some examination.

Consider, he says, the basic creation myths of the major religions. In Hinduism, the god Brahma is said to have created the world "through a kind of original sin"[7] — a mistake or error, one in which Brahma himself must atone for. (Schopenhauer adds with emphasis: "This is quite a good idea!") Buddhism, for its part, sees the world as coming into being "in consequence of an inexplicable disturbance in the crystal clearness of the blessed … state of Nirvana." ("An excellent idea!") The ancient Greeks saw the formation of the cosmos as an act of "unfathomable necessity," that which simply *had to be*. This too was reasonable. All such views saw the act of cosmic creation as a negation, as a failing — an error, a mistake, or an unfortunate necessity.

But the Judaic view was altogether different. There, the Jewish god Jehovah creates this world "of misery and woe," stands back on the seventh day, and declares it "all good" — what is this? Utter nonsense, declares Schopenhauer, and in fact "something intolerable." Recall the key passage from Genesis 1:31: "And God saw everything that he had made, and behold, it was very good." Schopenhauer repeatedly mocks this idea, drawing from and paraphrasing the Greek Septuagint version by use of the phrase πάντα καλὰ λίαν (pánta kalá lían),[8] "all was very good." This was pure nonsense, utterly disproven by common sense, philosophical insight, and even a modicum of a realist view of the world. Indeed, says Schopenhauer elsewhere, the world could hardly be any worse than it is.[9] To proclaim the opposite is sheer stupidity.

---

[6] *Parerga and Paralipomena* (hereafter, *P&P*), vol. 2, 315.

[7] *P&P*, vol. 2, 300.

[8] The full phrase in Genesis is: *kaí eíden o theós tá pánta ósa epoíisen kaí idoú kalá lían kaí egéneto espéra kaí egéneto proí iméra ékti.*

[9] "Now this world is arranged as it had to be, if it were to be capable of continuing with great difficulty to exist; if it were a little worse, it would no longer be capable of continuing to exist. Consequently, since a worse world could not continue to exist, it is absolutely impossible; and so this world itself is the worst of all possible worlds. …

As a putative religion, however, Judaism is even worse. There is a god in it, of course, but this deity is merely a brutal enforcer of the Law. He praises and cajoles his "chosen" and smites their enemies, nothing more. In this metaphysical system there is no immortal soul, no real afterlife, no heaven, no hell; all such things are utterly lacking in the Old Testament. Schopenhauer concludes,

> And so in this respect, we see the religion of the Jews occupy the lowest place among the dogmas of the civilized world, which is wholly in keeping with the fact that it is also the only religion that has absolutely no doctrine of immortality, nor has it even any trace thereof.[10]

Not that Schopenhauer endorsed the concept of an immortal soul; far from it. But he realized that any honest religion must include some such doctrine. Judaism, as we will see, evidently served a different purpose.

Nor did he accept anything like a moral, omnipotent, all-good god. "Such a view … is too flagrantly contradicted by the misery and wretchedness that fill the world, on the one hand, and by the obvious imperfection and even burlesque distortion of the most 'perfect' phenomenon … of man." The evil inherent in worldly existence, and the many failings of humanity, decisively disprove the existence of any such god. In fact, the great suffering of the world is proof of the opposite, namely, that it came into being in "sin," as the other religions have it. There remains a trace of this original sin, of course, in the Bible, in the myth of the Fall, of Adam and Eve—which stands as the only philosophically valid insight in Judaism: "it is only the story of the Fall of Man that reconciles me to the Old Testament. In fact, in my eyes, it is the only metaphysical truth that appears in the book."

Schopenhauer next turns to a central issue: the view of earthly life in the various religions. For emphasis, he contrasts the ancient Greek view with that of Christianity. Consider first the distinction between Greek and Christian views of death, as seen in images engraved on ancient sarcophagi. For the Greeks, the dead man's life is depicted in happy, optimistic terms: his birth, family, marriage, occupation, and so on. It is, says Schopenhauer, an essentially positive, *life-affirming* outlook; life is good, life is to be lived to its fullest, and people can indeed attain

---

Consequently, the world is as bad as it can possibly be, if it is to exist at all." (*WWE*, vol. 2, 583–584).

 [10] *P&P*, vol. 2, 301.

happiness. Then look at the Christian coffin: draped in black, and topped by the cross, the symbol of ultimate suffering and death. This, he said, is an essentially *life-denying* outlook. But it is fitting: for the Christian, this temporal life of sin and suffering is superseded by eternal life in heaven. What is life for a Christian, after all, but a test, a burden, indeed, a "cross to bear"?

From the perspective of a modern-day secular philosopher, one looks at this distinction and says: "Of course, the Greeks were right; you have one life, it can be good, so live it to the fullest. Those foolish Christians, with their mindless belief in an afterlife, disavow the value of earthly existence. They are always looking ahead, to heaven, never to the here and now." But Schopenhauer again turns the tables on us:

> Between the spirit of Graeco-Roman paganism and that of Christianity is the proper contrast of the affirmation and denial of the will-to-live, according to which, in the last resort, Christianity is fundamentally right.[11]

(I note here parenthetically that he frequently clarified his concept of the will as, more specifically, the will-to-live [*der Wille zum Leben*].) Christianity is "right" in the sense that the world *is* suffering, it *is* 'sin' — not for Christian reasons, of course, but because that is the nature of a world of pure willing. Even more, the Christian 'solution' is nearly the same as Schopenhauer's: *deny the will, be life-denying*. Will is will-to-live, and thus to deny the will is to deny life. Deny your material desires, deny bodily pleasures. Become an ascetic. "Take up your cross and follow me".[12] This is the path of redemption.

Hence Schopenhauer sees his philosophical worldview as aligned with the Christian New Testament and its 'pessimism' about the world, whereas other philosophers are inherently more consistent with the 'optimistic' view of Judaism and the Old Testament:

> My ethics is related to all the ethical systems of European philosophy as the New Testament to the Old, according to the ecclesiastical conception of this relation. Thus the Old Testament puts man under the authority of the Law [of Moses] which, however, does *not* lead to salvation. The New Testament, on the other hand, declares the

---

[11] *P&P*, vol. 2, 314.
[12] Mark 8:34; Matthew 16:24.

Law to be inadequate, in fact repudiates it. On the contrary, it preaches the kingdom of grace which is attained by faith, love of one's neighbor, and complete denial of oneself; this is the path to salvation from evil and the world. For in spite of all protestant-rationalistic distortions and misrepresentations, the ascetic spirit is assuredly and quite properly the soul of the New Testament. But this is just the denial of the will-to-live. ...

He then places his own outlook in historical context:

Now all the philosophical systems of ethics prior to mine have kept to the spirit of the Old Testament, with their absolute moral law and all their moral commandments and prohibitions, to which the commanding Jehovah is secretly added in thought. ... My ethics, on the other hand, ... frankly and sincerely admits the abominable nature of the world, and points to the denial of the will as the path to redemption therefrom. It is, accordingly, actually in the spirit of the New Testament, whereas all the others are in that of the Old, and thus theoretically amount to mere Judaism (plain despotic theism). In this sense, my teaching could be called Christian philosophy proper, paradoxical as this may seem to those who do not go to the root of the matter, but stick merely to the surface.[13]

Thus arriving back at the quotation I cited above. Judaism, with its *pánta kalá lían*, an all-good God, and a promise of material prosperity, is a pathetic form of optimism, utterly at odds with the real world. (Of course, for the Jews themselves over the past century at least, and excepting a few years during WW2, the world has been exceptionally good; it's good to be king. I will return to this shortly.) Christianity, with its sufferings of the world, its sin and misery and death, and its "you will be hated by all",[14] is realistic pessimism—albeit, as with Schopenhauer, with an escape route, namely, denial of the will and the consequent asceticism. The analogy is imperfect but sufficient to allow for an instructive comparison. It permitted Schopenhauer to draw out some fascinating implications but it also blinded him to a likely deeper truth about Christianity.

---

[13] *P&P*, vol. 2, 314.
[14] Matthew 10:22, Luke 6:22, John 15:19.

SEXUAL ABSTINENCE AS JEWISH ETHNIC STRATEGY

Among many other things, Schopenhauer was fascinated by human sexuality, which for him assumed deep metaphysical importance. The human essence, the will-to-live, finds "as its kernel and greatest concentration, the act of generation" — which is to say, sexual reproduction. Here is the beginning of everything, not only of biology but of the whole great charade that is human existence. With a biting sense of humor, he explains it this way:

> Seriously speaking, this is due to the fact that sexual desire, especially when, through fixation on a definite woman, it is concentrated to amorous infatuation, is the quintessence of the whole fraud of this noble world; for it promises so unspeakably, infinitely, and excessively much, and then performs so contemptibly little.[15]

Appropriately, then, sexual desire is the prime urging that must be suppressed by any real ascetic. Hence, by rights, we should find this admonition in the New Testament; and in fact, we do. Schopenhauer examines this matter in his exceptionally important Chapter 48 of Volume Two of *World as Will and Representation*:

> The ascetic tendency is certainly unmistakable in genuine and original Christianity. … We find, as its principal teaching, the recommendation of genuine and pure celibacy (that first and most important step in the denial of the will-to-live) already expressed in the New Testament.[16]

And he means, not only for single men and women, *but for the married as well*. Schopenhauer's astonishing claim, that he proceeds to adduce from primary evidence, is that *good Christians should not have sex — ever*. He then dedicates the next several pages to building his case for this "perpetual chastity," which includes these lines from an 1832 book by the Catholic author Friedrich Carove:

> By virtue of the Church view … perpetual chastity is called a divine, heavenly, angelic virtue. … [Quoting a Catholic periodical,] "In Catholicism, the observance of a perpetual chastity, for God's sake, appears in itself as the highest merit of man." … To both [Paul and the

---

[15] *P&P*, vol. 2, 316.
[16] *WWE*, vol. 2, 616.

author of Hebrews], virginity was perfection, marriage only a make-shift for the weaker. ... The self should turn away and refrain from everything that contributes only to its pleasure. ... We agree with Abbe Zaccaria, who asserts that celibacy ... is derived above all from the teaching of Christ and of the Apostle Paul.[17]

At this point we want to exclaim: Can this be true? Could original Christianity actually expect its followers to adhere to "perpetual chastity," even when married? And what would prompt such a call?

Evidence for this claim must ultimately come from our primary source, the New Testament. We further know that the earliest NT writings are the letters of Paul, which predate the four Gospels by two or three decades, at least. Let's briefly look at the evidence, both that which Schopenhauer offers and that which we may supplement on our own.

Schopenhauer cites two passages from Paul. The first and earliest is 1 Thessalonians (4:3), an oddly cryptic passage. Paul says, "For it is the will of God, for your sanctification, that you abstain from *porneias*." I cite here the Greek original—but what is *porneias*? Among the 70-odd English translations we find a range of terms, such as "immorality" (RSV), "sexual immorality" (NKJV), and "fornication" (KJV), all of which suggest illegitimate sex, perhaps unmarried sex, perhaps adultery. But we also find broader terms, like "all sexual vice" (AMPC), "sexual sins" (ERV), "sexual defilement" (TPT), and even "unchastity" (RSV). Paul goes on to say that "each one of you knows how to take a wife in holiness and honor, not in the passion of lust like a heathen." Can he be suggesting that men take wives as "partners in Christ" all while abstaining from the sexual lust of heathens?

The second passage is a lengthy portion from 1 Corinthians 7. Again, it is oddly conflicted. At the start of the chapter, Paul says, bluntly, "It is good for a man not to have sexual relations with a woman" (7:1, ESV). But owing to "the temptation to immorality"—presumably meaning sexual intercourse—a man may take a wife. Affirming his own unmarried status, Paul then says "I wish that all were as I myself am. ... To the unmarried and the widows, I say that it is well for them to remain single as I do" (7:7-8). "But if they cannot exercise self-control"—that is, if they are weak—"they should marry." Later in the chapter, Paul returns to the subject: "Are you free from a wife? Do not seek marriage" (7:27). Two lines later he warns, "those who marry will have worldly troubles (!), and I

---

[17] *WWE*, vol. 2, 619–620.

would spare you that." Paul goes on to state that married people are worried about worldly matters and about pleasing each other, which distracts them from their "undivided devotion to the Lord." A married man may do well, says Paul, "but he who refrains from marriage will do better" (7:38). These are striking words from our "Apostle." It seems clear — Paul will accept you if you marry, but he would much prefer that you did not.

There are other Pauline passages that Schopenhauer might have cited. For example, Colossians 3:5: "Put to death, therefore, whatever belongs to your earthly nature: sexual immorality, impurity, lust, evil desires and greed, which is idolatry" (NIV). Or Galatians 5:16-19: "Do not gratify the desires of the flesh. For the desires of the flesh are against the Spirit. ... The acts of the flesh are obvious: sexual immorality, impurity and debauchery." Or 1 Corinthians 6:18: "Flee from sexual immorality. All other sins a person commits are outside the body, but whoever sins sexually, sins against their own body." Or Romans 13:14: "Rather, clothe yourselves with the Lord Jesus Christ, and do not think about how to gratify the desires of the flesh." We might also include the pseudepigraphic Ephesians 5:3: "But among you there must not be even a hint of sexual immorality, or of any kind of impurity, or of greed, because these are improper for God's holy people." This is prudish Puritanism in the extreme. Paul, indeed, seems to strongly prefer that his fellow Christians have no sexual relations at all.

There are other related suggestions in the Gospels. Schopenhauer refers to Matthew 19:10, where the disciples offer to Jesus the idea that "perhaps it is better not to marry." Jesus gives a typically cryptic reply, suggesting that chastity may be best:

> Not everyone can accept this word, but only those to whom it has been given. For there are eunuchs who were born that way, and there are eunuchs who have been made eunuchs by others — and there are those who choose to live like eunuchs for the sake of the kingdom of heaven. The one who can accept this should accept it.

The apparent suggestion here is that we all should 'be like a eunuch,' and not have sex. In Luke 20:34 Jesus addresses the future resurrection of married people: "The people of this age marry and are given in marriage. But those who are considered worthy of taking part in the age to come, and in the resurrection from the dead, will neither marry nor be given in marriage." Indeed, the unmarried are "equal to angels and are sons of God." It's clear who the preferred people are.

Outside the Gospels and the Pauline Epistles, we have 1 John 2:15: "Do not love the world or the things in the world. ... For all that is in the world, the lust of the flesh and the lust of the eyes, is not of the Father but is of the world." Or we could cite 1 Peter 2:11: "Beloved, I urge you as aliens and exiles to abstain from the desires of the flesh that wage war against the soul" (NSRV). And in the late-written Revelations, we read that the Lamb of God will return to Earth only with those "who have not defiled themselves with women, for they are chaste" (14:4).

What is one to conclude? It seems that Schopenhauer is right—that perpetual chastity is the prescribed course of action for all good Christians.

But why? Why would Paul, for example, encourage his would-be followers to abstain from sex? Obviously he did not get this suggestion from "Jesus" or from God; it was clearly his own doing. Obviously he did not get it from the Old Testament, with its many calls to "be fruitful and multiply".[18] The idea itself of a celibate religious group was not unknown to him, as it was characteristic of a number of esoteric cults and secretive groups over the centuries. But Paul wasn't aiming at some clandestine cult; he wanted a mass movement. He must have known that it was poor organizational strategy to ask people to commit to chastity. Clearly he had some compelling reason for introducing this component into his new religion.

Schopenhauer had no real knowledge of evolution, having been born a few decades too early, and so it is understandable that he had no idea of group evolutionary strategy. If he had, he might have discerned something in Paul's motive—an overriding concern for the welfare of his fellow Jews. As an elite Pharisee Jew, Paul (born Saul) clearly resented the incursion of the Roman Empire into Palestine, in the decades prior to his birth. He also surely shared the long-standing Jewish antipathy for his neighboring Gentile masses—Arabs, Greeks, and Egyptians.[19] Seeing the futility of violent resistance to Rome, Paul was surely searching for non-violent, indirect, psychological or moral means of undermining the

---

[18] Genesis 1:28, 9:1, 9:7, 17:20, 28:3, 35:11; Exodus 1:7; Leviticus 26:9; Jeremiah 23:3.

[19] Jewish misanthropy is notorious and well-documented. It dates back at least to Hecateus of Abdera, *circa* 300 BC, who observed that "Moses introduced a way of life [for the Jews] which was to a certain extent misanthropic and hostile to foreigners." Apollonius Molon, *circa* 75 BC, "reviled the Jews as atheists and misanthropes." In 50 BC, Diodorus Siculus remarked that "the nation of Jews had made their hatred of mankind into a tradition." The list of such commentaries is extensive; for details, see my work *Eternal Strangers* (Uckfield, U.K.: Castle Hill, 2020).

enemy. Then he hit upon a plan: Why not play up the alleged divinity of a recently-crucified Jewish rabbi, Jesus of Nazareth, turning him into the savior of all humanity? This way, all of Paul's exhortations—in his self-assigned role as "Apostle to the Gentiles"—could be turned into an anti-Gentile morality and placed into the mouth of God himself. 'It's not my idea,' implies Paul; 'God wants you to be chaste—forever.'

But is "perpetual chastity" anti-Gentile? Yes—if, by proscribing future children, it erodes Gentile families. This, in fact, is the only practical consequence: fewer Gentile children. Seen this way, as a Jewish ethnic evolutionary strategy, Paul found a way to inhibit the growth of the non-Jewish population. If there is any historical basis to the concept of "White genocide," this is it.

And it wasn't only Paul. Above I gave two chastity quotations from the Gospels of Matthew and Luke. Those same two books also contain, unsurprisingly, a number of explicitly anti-family passages. In Matthew 10:21, Jesus says, "Brother will betray brother to death, and a father his child; children will rebel against their parents and have them put to death." At Matthew 19:29, Jesus proclaims, "And everyone who has left houses or brothers or sisters or father or mother or wife or children or fields for my sake will receive a hundred times as much, and will inherit eternal life." In the Gospel of Luke (12:52) we read, "From now on, there will be five in one family divided against each other, three against two and two against three." And later (14:26) we find that Jesus says, "If anyone comes to me and does not hate father and mother, wife and children, brothers and sisters—yes, even their own life—such a person cannot be my disciple." What is this but a family-destroying message, an admonition to tear apart familial ties, all while staying chaste, simply for the sake of "Jesus"? The Jewish Gospel writers seem to have clearly endorsed Paul's anti-Gentile strategy.

In the end, of course, this anti-family stance had to be abandoned, as Schopenhauer makes clear. Beginning with Clement of Alexandria, *circa* 200 AD—especially in book 3 of his *Stromata*—Gentile Christian Fathers rejected the anti-marriage, anti-family, and anti-child stance of the early Jewish Christians. Clement rails against earlier Fathers like Marcion and Tatian, who held to the literal, anti-natalist reading: "they teach that one should not enter into matrimony and beget children, should not bring further unhappy beings into the world, and produce fresh fodder for death".[20] Writing two centuries later, Augustine too recognized this

---

[20] Cited by Schopenhauer in *WWE*, vol. 2, 622 note.

dilemma in the early Christian Fathers: "They reject marriage and put it on a level with fornication and other vices." By way of modest defense, and with perhaps a touch of irony, he adds that, with mass abstention, "the kingdom of God would be realized far more quickly, since the end of the world would be hastened".[21]

Still, it was clear that mass perpetual chastity was not a practical way to build a worldwide religion, and in the end it had to be abandoned or "reinterpreted" by Catholics and Protestants alike. They had to adopt the Jewish optimism, the *pánta kalá lían,* and surrender the central aspect of Christian asceticism, its perpetual chastity. But in doing so, they drained away the key elements of their own religion. As Schopenhauer says, summing up the situation, "From all this, it seems to me that Catholicism is a disgracefully abused, and Protestantism a degenerate, Christianity".[22]

ON THE JEWS

Where, then, does all this leave us? For Schopenhauer, Christianity had an original and profound core in its inherently life-denying outlook, something which was consistent with his own philosophical stance. But it got subverted and contaminated with the detestable Jewish optimism, and thus lost to history. For all his skepticism, Schopenhauer seems to believe that an historical (but non-miraculous) Jesus really existed, and that Paul was an honest interpreter of his message. In retrospect, this seems utterly naïve. Far more likely is that Paul and the Jewish Gospel writers were master deceivers—"artful liars," as Hitler might have put it[23]—who were only interested in Jewish power and Jewish well-being, and who thus instituted an effective Jewish group-strategy to confuse and weaken the Gentile masses. And in the end, and even though some aspects had to be jettisoned, it worked. Rome collapsed and Christianity went global. Given that we have some 2 billion Christians on Earth today, the implications are enormous.

Schopenhauer's many reflections on religion, and his negative assessment of Judaism in particular, furthermore allowed him the opportunity to offer a number of critical comments on Jews generally. Even in his early writing, in volume one of *World as Will and Representation,* he offered harsh

---

[21] Cited in *WWE,* vol. 2, 618 note.

[22] *WWE,* vol. 2, 626.

[23] In *Mein Kampf,* vol. 1, section 2.25, Hitler expresses his amazement at the Jews' "art of lying" (*Kunst der Lüge*). And later in chapter 10 (section 10.4), he employs the explicit phrase "artful liars" (*Lügenkünstler*). See my new translation (New York: Clemens & Blair, 2017).

commentary. In a passage on the development of the arts, he briefly addresses "the history of a small, isolated, capricious, hierarchical (i.e. ruled by false notions), obscure people, like the Jews, despised by the great contemporary nations of the East and of the West".[24] "It is to be regarded generally as a great misfortune," he adds, "that the people whose former culture was to serve mainly as the basis of our own were not, say, the Indians or the Greeks, or even the Romans, but just these Jews."

For the next three decades, he said little about them. But he returned to the topic, in a very pointed manner, in *Parerga and Paralipomena*. Volume 1 begins with a sketch of the history of idealism and the limitations of that metaphysical view. The classic idealists are closely allied with Judeo-Christian theology, and thus "are all marred by that Jewish theism which is impervious to any investigation, dead to all research, and thus actually appears as a fixed idea".[25] But the subsequent essay, on the history of philosophy, brings the occasion for an extended digression on the subject:

> The real religion of the Jews, as presented and taught in Genesis and all the historical books up to the end of Chronicles, is the crudest of all religions because it is the only one that has absolutely no doctrine of immortality, not even a trace thereof. ... The contempt in which the Jews were always held by contemporary peoples may have been due in great measure to the poor character of their religion. ... Now this wretched religion of the Jews does not [offer any conception of an afterlife], in fact it does not even attempt it. It is, therefore, the crudest and poorest of all religions and consists merely in an absurd and revolting theism. ... While all other religions endeavor to explain to the people by symbols and parables the metaphysical significance of life, the religion of the Jews is entirely immanent, and furnishes nothing but a mere war-cry in the struggle with other nations.[26]

Here we see real insight: Judaism is not a religion at all, but rather a war-manual in the competition with other peoples. It serves to sustain and promote the Jewish race in their material well-being, nothing more.

Volume 2 elaborates on these ideas, especially in the chapter titled "On Religion," which brings this observation:

---

[24] *WWE*, vol. 1, 232.

[25] *P&P*, vol. 1, 15.

[26] *P&P*, vol. 1, 125–126.

Also we should not forget God's chosen people who, after they had stolen, by Jehovah's express command, the gold and silver vessels lent to them by their old and trusty friends in Egypt, now made their murderous and predatory attack on the 'Promised Land,' with the murderer Moses at their head, in order to tear away from the rightful owners, by the same Jehovah's express and constantly repeated command, showing no mercy, and ruthlessly murdering and exterminating all the inhabitants, even the women and children.[27]

A footnote to the above passage adds this widely-cited remark:

Tacitus and Justinus have handed down to us the historical basis of the Exodus. … We see from the two Roman authors how much the Jews were at all times and by all nations loathed and despised. This may be partly due to the fact that they were the only people on earth who did not credit man with any existence beyond this life and were, therefore, regarded as beasts. … Scum of humanity — but great master of lies [*grosse Meister im Lügen*].[28]

The ultimate tragedy, for Schopenhauer, is that the pathetic *Judeo-Christian* culture dominated the history of Europe, rather than the nobler Greco-Roman: "The religion of the Greeks and Romans, those world-powers, has perished. The religion of the contemptible little Jewish race [*verachteten Judenvölkchens*], on the other hand, has been preserved.[29]

But, as noted, the Hebrew tribe is not simply defined by a religion; "it is an extremely superficial and false view to regard the Jews merely as a religious sect. … On the contrary, 'Jewish Nation' is the correct expression".[30] Like Johann Fichte and Johann Herder, Schopenhauer was also concerned about the political consequences of integrating, and granting rights to, this Jewish Nation. The Jews were a "*gens extorris*" (refugee race), eternally uprooted, always searching for but never finding a homeland:

---

[27] *P&P*, vol. 2, 357.

[28] Payne mistranslates this sentence, interpreting the final phrase as "past master at telling lies."

[29] *P&P*, vol. 2, 393.

[30] *P&P*, vol. 2, 263.

Till then, it lives parasitically on other nations and their soil; but yet it is inspired with the liveliest patriotism for its own nation. This is seen in the very firm way in which Jews stick together ... and no community on earth sticks so firmly together as does this. It follows that it is absurd to want to concede to them a share in the government or administration of any country.[31]

Schopenhauer was more moderate than Fichte; banishment was not necessary. He was willing to grant them limited rights, *provided* they took no role in government. "Justice demands that they should enjoy with others equal civil rights; but to concede to them a share in the running of the State is absurd. They are and remain a foreign oriental race."[32] ... The race could be tolerated, but the corrupt ideology had to go: "We may therefore hope that one day even Europe will be purified of all Jewish mythology."[33]

Finally, Schopenhauer found much use in an intriguing little phrase, *foetor Judaicus* — the 'Jewish stench.' For him, the stench represents not so much a literal smell but rather an intellectual odor of stale Jewish thought, arising primarily from the Old Testament. Oddly enough, he applies it most often in his critique of Jewish approaches to animal rights.[34] In the *Parerga* he criticizes Spinoza (and his view of animals) as a man who speaks "just as a Jew knows how to do, so that we others, who are accustomed to purer and worthier doctrines, are here overcome by the *foetor Judaicus*".[35] Of the Genesis account that God created animals for man's use, Schopenhauer exclaims, "Such stories have on me the same effect as do Jew's pitch and *foetor Judaicus!*"[36] Somewhat later he refers to "Europe, the continent that is so permeated with the *foetor Judaicus*."[37] And on the same subject: "It is obviously high time that in Europe, Jewish views on nature were brought to an end. ... A man must be bereft of all his senses or completely chloroformed by the *foetor Judaicus* not to see [this]."[38]

---

[31] *P&P*, vol. 2, 262.

[32] *P&P*, vol. 2, 264.

[33] *P&P*, vol. 2, 226.

[34] Schopenhauer was a passionate advocate for animal welfare, far ahead of his time on that count. He was the first major philosopher to incorporate them into his ethical schema.

[35] *P&P*, vol. 1, 73.

[36] *P&P*, vol. 2, 370. "Jew's pitch" is a naturally-occurring bituminous asphalt, found in ancient times around the Dead Sea and other parts of Judea.

[37] *P&P*, vol. 2, 372.

[38] *P&P*, vol. 2, 375.

Members of the alt-right, no longer "chloroformed by the *foetor Judaicus*" nor deceived by the "great master of lies," can see the evident truth in such statements—statements that were years ahead of their time, and written in a period when a great thinker could still speak the truth. Sadly, and thanks to Jewish domination of our society, we can no longer openly say such things without harsh recriminations. True free speech no longer exists. Hence we are locked into a long struggle with the Jewish race, simply to achieve basic freedoms of speech and expression, and to live our lives out from under the dominance of the Jewish hand.

Perhaps this is our lot in life—and indeed, the lot of all people everywhere. This calls to mind a well-known quotation from Schopenhauer, which I cite here in context:

> History shows us the life of nations and can find nothing to relate except wars and insurrections; the years of peace appear here and there only as short pauses, as intervals between the acts. And in the same way, the life of the individual is a perpetual struggle, not merely metaphorically with want or boredom, but actually with others. Everywhere he finds an opponent, lives in constant conflict, and dies weapon in hand.[39]

Less known is that the concluding thought appears earlier in the book, in different form, and is attributed to Voltaire. The words are apt:

> In this world where "the dice are loaded," we need a temper of iron, armor against fate, and weapons against mankind. For the whole of life is a struggle, every step contested, and Voltaire rightly says, *on ne réussit dans ce monde qu'à la pointe de l'épée, et on meurt les armes à la main* ("In this world, we succeed only at the point of the sword, and we die with weapons in hand.")[40]

In such a world, says Schopenhauer, our motto should be (quoting Virgil): *tu ne cede malis, sed contra audentior ito* ("Do not give way to evil, but face it more boldly"—*Aeneid* 6.95). The situation demands courage and resolve; "we should not think of nervousness or hesitation, but only of resistance." We must harden ourselves, and stiffen our resolve; he cites Horace: *Si fractus illabatur orbis, Impavidum ferient ruinae* ("Even if the world collapses over a man, the ruins still leave him undismayed"—*Odes*

---

[39] *P&P*, vol. 2, 292.

[40] *P&P*, vol. 1, 475. Original source for Voltaire is *Les pensées et maximes* (1821).

III, 3.7). The future is there for those who are willing to face the battle head-on: *Quocirca vivite fortes, Fortiaque adversis opponite pectora rebus* ("Therefore he lives bravely and presents a bold front to the blows of fate" — *Satires* II, 2.135). As they say, timeless wisdom is eternally valuable.

But perhaps we leave the last word to Schopenhauer himself. His pessimistic realism held true to the end. In volume two of the *Parerga*, he sums up all the strivings of our lives:

> A happy life is impossible; the best that man can attain is a *heroic life*, such as is lived by one who struggles against overwhelming odds in some way and in some affair that will benefit the whole of mankind, and who, in the end, triumphs — although he obtains a poor reward, or none at all.[41]

The message is clear: Have low expectations of life; as a rule, things will not go as we wish. Any victories will be rare, hard-fought, fleeting, and unacknowledged. Life is perpetual struggle; therefore, never give up. Above all, strive to be heroic.

Words to ponder, for all those who would fight for justice in this unjust world.

Thomas Dalton, PhD, is a professor of humanities at a major American university. He has authored or edited several books and articles on politics, history, and religion, with a special focus on the National Socialist era in Germany. He has also conducted extensive research on historical and contemporary Jewish relations. His most recent works include Debating the Holocaust *(4th ed),* Eternal Strangers, The Jewish Hand in the World Wars, *and a new translation of* Mein Kampf. *Details of his work can be found at http://www.thomasdaltonphd.com.*

---

[41] *P&P*, vol. 2, 322.

RECENT ADVANCES IN THE SCIENCE OF HUMAN DIFFERENCES

Human Diversity:
The Biology of Gender, Race, and Class
by Charles Murray
New York: Grand Central Publishing, 2020

Reviewed by F. Roger Devlin

"We are in the midst of a uniquely exciting period of discoveries in genetics and neuroscience (6)," notes Charles Murray near the beginning of his latest book *Human Diversity*, yet it remains something of a secret. Knowledgeable specialists avoid publicizing the discoveries, frequently claiming to be afraid the information will be misinterpreted and misused (i.e., by "White supremacists" and such). What they are really afraid of is retaliation by an aggressive minority of their colleagues who enforce a scientifically unsupported orthodoxy that Murray sums up in three assertions:

> 1) *Gender is a social construct.* Physiological sex differences associated with childbearing have been used to create artificial gender roles that are unjustified by inborn characteristics of personality, abilities, or social behavior.
> 2) *Race is a social construct.* The concept of race has arisen from cosmetic differences in appearance that are not accompanied by inborn differences in personality, abilities, or social behavior
> 3) *Class is a function of privilege.* People have historically been sorted into classes by political, economic, and cultural institutions that privilege heterosexual white males and oppress everyone else, with genes and human nature playing a trivial role if any. People can be resorted in a socially just way by changing these institutions. (3)

This orthodoxy has been on the defensive for many years now, and Murray is optimistic it will collapse within the coming decade. Plenty of individual believers will remain, but collectively they will lose their ability to enforce their beliefs through intimidation.

Human Diversity is a report on the revolution in our understanding of race, sex and class differences over the last thirty years. The author draws on genetic advances made possible by the sequencing of the human genome and also on neuroscience, but avoids extensive appeals to evolutionary psychology: "I decided that incorporating its insights would make it too easy for critics to attack the explanation and ignore the empirical reality." (7)

This is part of a strategy "to stick to the low-hanging fruit" of findings "that have broad acceptance within their disciplines," even if it leaves expert readers "yawning with boredom." (6) Though soft-spoken by nature, Murray clearly hopes to strike an unanswerable blow against the Lysenkoist mafia whose power he has experienced personally. He conveniently summarizes his basic message in ten propositions for which "the clamor of genuine scientific dispute has abated," (7) and there is little room left for empirically informed dispute. The first four propositions deal with sex differences, the next three with race, and the last three with class. Each proposition is given a chapter of its own.

THE REALITY OF SEX DIFFERENCES

The first proposition states that sex differences in personality are consistent worldwide and tend to widen in more gender-egalitarian cultures. Few will be surprised to find the latest studies confirming that women tend toward the warm, sympathetic, accommodating, altruistic and sociable end of the personality scale, with men more inclined to be reserved, utilitarian, unsentimental, dispassionate and solitary. Such differences emerge early in life are found around the world in radically different cultural environments.

A more counterintuitive finding is that such sex differences in personality widen rather than diminish in more egalitarian countries: this was the consistent result of five extensive international studies published between 2001 and 2018. As Murray notes, social constructivists are not the only ones surprised by this: "I know of no ideological perspective that would have predicted greater sex differences in personality in Scandinavia than in Africa or Asia." He offers the conjecture that stronger enforcement of social norms in more traditional societies may suppress the expression of inborn personality traits, while in the modern West the sexes are "freer to do what comes naturally." (43)

The second proposition states that "on average, females worldwide have advantages in verbal ability and social cognition while males have advantages in visuospatial abilities and the extremes of mathematical ability." Social cognition refers to the ability to infer mental states from external clues and predict other people's intentions and reactions. Women's superior verbal skills are a consistent finding of international student assessment tests. Women also have better sensory perception and fine motor skills, and are better than men at remembering the minutiae (peripheral detail) of events.

Men are better at remembering the gist, and have markedly superior visuospatial skills. There has also long existed a widespread perception that men are better at math than women. Recent evidence makes some qualification necessary. Within the normal ability range, the male advantage is not statistically significant. It is clearer at the high end, but even here diminished greatly during the 1980s. Among the top one percent of one percent of human mathematical ability, there were 13 boys for every girl in the 1970s; by the early 1990s, the ratio had sunk to 3 to 1, where it has remained stable ever since.

Even where men and women solve problems equally well, they may do so in different ways. For example, women tend to navigate by identifying and remembering landmarks, while men are more likely to construct mental maps. Women more often use verbal forms of logic to solve math problems, whereas men tend to use symbolic or spatial reasoning.

Among the most cherished of feminist beliefs is that female under-representation in STEM fields (science, technology, engineering and math) reflects differences in socialization, and would disappear in a gender-neutral society. To test this hypothesis, Murray examines the preferences and choices of a cohort chosen for a Johns Hopkins Study of Mathematically Precocious Youth (SMPY). Focusing on such a sample allows him to ignore sex differences in abilities: all these people were qualified to pursue any undergraduate major they liked.

In the upper-middle-class schools and neighborhoods where most of the SMPY girls grew up, courses were filled with inspirational stories about women scientists, political leaders, artists, and authors. High schools were putting boys and girls in the same gym classes, and high school counselors were urging female students to go into male-dominated careers. When they reached college age in 1982-5, they all knew that the most famous universities in the nation were eager to add them to their student bodies and even more eager for them to populate their majors in science, technology, engineering, and math. On campuses, young women were hearing faculty and their fellow students urging them to forgo marriage and childbearing in favor of a career. (72)

It would not be easy to find a hypothesis which has been given a fairer or larger-scale trial than the explanation of female underrepresentation in STEM fields by sex-specific socialization.

The SMPY women were, indeed, about twice as likely as women in the general population to major in STEM subjects—but so were the men, so that the sex ratio was about the same. Twice as many of the women got degrees in the social sciences, business, and the humanities as did the men. Those of the women who did major in STEM subjects inclined more to the life sciences rather than math or the physical sciences.

An important reason for the persistent underrepresentation of women in STEM fields even among the mathematically gifted elite may be that many of these women *also* enjoyed their sex's natural advantage in verbal intelligence, giving them "an attractive array of alternatives to STEM" (78)—whereas the men's intelligence was more likely to skew heavily toward mathematics.

In 2012–13 a team of Vanderbilt psychologists interviewed these SMPY men and women, by then in their late forties, about their work preferences. The women indicated a much greater willingness to consider part-time careers and a greater unwillingness to work more than forty hours a week. They sought flexibility in their work schedule and placed a high value on such things as "having strong friendships." Murray notes that since these women were in their late forties, their preference for shorter hours and a flexible schedule was not likely to be due to the presence of small children at home.

The men expressed a strong preference for a full-time career with a high salary, and agreed with such statements as "The prospect of receiving criticism from others does not inhibit me from expressing my thoughts' and "I believe society should invest in my ideas because they are more important than those of other people in my discipline." They viewed "being able to take risks on my job" as a positive good, and reported that they enjoyed working with computers, tools and machines.

In short, the stated preferences of these highly talented men and women who had come of age at the height of the feminist educational and career revolution were utterly sex-typical. Yet their widely differing preferences "were not accompanied by corresponding sex differences in how they viewed their career accomplishments and close relationships, or in their positive outlook on life," according to the Vanderbilt researchers.

(76) Forcing statistically equal life outcomes on the women in this sample might have been possible under totalitarian conditions, but would almost certainly have left them less happy.

The patterns observed in this cohort of unusually talented men and women holds for people general. Consider, for example, the RIASEC psychological assessment battery widely used for career guidance: of the six dimensions of preferences and abilities it measures, two reveal large and consistent sex differences. Those who score highest on the trait labelled "Realistic" enjoy working with tools, instruments, and mechanical or electrical equipment, as well as activities such as building, repairing machinery, and raising crops or animals. Men are higher on this measure by 84 percent of a standard deviation. Those who score highest on the trait labeled "Social" enjoy helping, enlightening or serving others through activities such as teaching, counseling, working in service-oriented organizations and engaging in social and political studies. Women are higher on this measure by 68 percent of a standard deviation. And these differences do not just show up in career assessment tests, but are closely mirrored by the actual jobs men and women go on to hold.

All of this evidence goes to confirm an observation made in 1911 by Edward Thorndike, a founder of the discipline of educational psychology, that the greatest cognitive difference between men and women lies "in the relative strength of their interest in things and their mechanisms (stronger in men) and the interest in persons and their feelings (stronger in women)." (19-20) This provided the inspiration for the third proposition: "on average, women worldwide are more attracted to vocations centered on people and men to vocations centered on things."

Murray notes that in the late 1980s, observers could have been forgiven for predicting that the career preferences of men and women

> would converge within a few decades. From 1970 through the mid-1980s, the percentage of women in Things jobs had risen and the male-female ratio had plunged. If those [trends] had been sustained, the percentages of men and women in Things jobs would have intersected around 2001. But convergence was already slowing by the late 1980s and had effectively stalled by 1990. (87)

For example, between 1971 and 1986, the percentage of women's bachelor of science degrees in the most things-oriented STEM fields — physics, chemistry, earth sciences, computer sciences, mathematics and engineering — more than doubled, but from a base of only 4 percent to a high of 10 percent. By 1992 it had declined again to 6 percent, where it has remained ever since, give or take a percentage point. The author concludes:

> It looks as if women were indeed artificially constrained from moving into a variety of Things occupations as of 1970, that those constraints were largely removed, and that equilibrium was reached around 30 years ago. (88)

The fourth proposition states that "many sex differences in the brain are coordinate with sex differences in personality, abilities and behavior." As neurological researcher Larry Cahill wrote in 2017: "The past 15 to 20 years witnesses an explosion of research documenting sex influences at all levels of brain function. So overpowering is the wave of research that the standard ways of dismissing sex influences have all been swept away." Some of the most obvious sex differences in temperament are due to sex hormones, of which testosterone and estrogen are the best known (there are many others). Both men and women produce both of these hormones, but men produce much more testosterone and women much more estrogen.

Studies have demonstrated that a single dose of testosterone administered to women

> significantly altered connectivity of the network in the brain that underlies the integration and selection of sensory information during empathic behavior. This finding suggests a neural mechanism by which testosterone can impair the recognition of emotions. (100)

The administration of testosterone has also been found to diminish women's accuracy in inferring mental states, and women with higher natural levels of testosterone have been observed to be less risk-averse than other women. Supplemental testosterone administered to men diminishes their performance on the Cognitive Reflection Test, which measures capacity to override intuitive judgments with deliberated answers. Estrogen administered to men increases their emotional response to watching a distressed person.

Among the most important but less widely known functions of testosterone is to masculinize the fetal brain. Testosterone surges in human males occur twice before birth, during weeks 12–18 and again during weeks 34–41; a third occurs in the first three months after birth. In the absence of these testosterone surges, the brain develops according to the

female pattern, which is thus in some sense the "default" type of human brain.

Since this discovery was made in 1959, many experiments have been conducted on nonhuman mammals in which hormones are manipulated during critical periods of prenatal and neonatal development. It has been established that certain regions of the brain have receptors which accept chemical signals from hormones. These signals affect a cell's anatomical connectivity and neurochemicals, and even whether it survives or not.

Complete androgen insensitivity syndrome (CAIS) is a rare but instructive disorder that affects genetically male humans, i.e., persons with a Y chromosome. Such persons produce normal amounts of testosterone at the proper time — but to no effect, because their androgen receptors do not work. Persons with CAIS are born with externally normal female genitalia, are reared as girls, and are in *most* respects indistinguishable from girls behaviorally.

A 2017 Swedish study identified many specific ways in which fetuses with a Y chromosome but affected by CAIS develop brains that are a mix of characteristically "male" and "female" patterns. To give just one example: they are characteristically female with regard to hippocampus volume and male with regard to caudate volume. The study concluded that similarities in brain structure between the CAIS women and female controls are due to the CAIS condition, while similarities with male controls were due to the effects of their Y chromosome.

A few defenders of feminist orthodoxy have written books critical of hormone research, and been rewarded with "uniformly and sometimes gushingly enthusiastic … reviews in the mainstream press," according to Murray. (106) But the best that can be said for their critiques is that they have succeeded in pointing out how some research has fallen short of perfection due to "small samples, inconsistent results, and scarce replications." (105) But neuroscientists have not put much effort into refuting these books, apart from a few of them "having had scathing things to say in blogs." One researcher told Murray that "one reason you don't find many critiques … is that people in the field really don't care. It's so evidently nonsense." (106) In short, empirically oriented scientists live in a largely separate mental world from the armchair theorists of social constructivism.

Among the best attested neurological sex differences is the greater "laterality" of the male brain, meaning that it is "structurally optimized for communicating within hemispheres" (112) as a result of fetal masculinization. The female brain is optimized for communication across hemispheres: the corpus callosum, which connects the two hemispheres is thicker in women, even after controlling for brain size and age. Men primarily use their right hemisphere for spatial tasks and their left hemisphere for verbal tasks, while women use both hemispheres for both.

> When women suffer brain damage to the left hemisphere, they are less likely than men to develop language difficulties. Women's language test scores after brain damage suffer the same effect whether the damage occurred to the left or right hemisphere, whereas men are more affected by damage to the left hemisphere. (110)

A recent study found that males have greater connectivity between the motor and sensory systems, and in systems associated with complex reasoning and control. Females have higher connectivity with the subcortical regions associated with emotion processing. Researchers say these results "suggest a better perception-action coordination in males, and better anticipation and subsequent processing of socially and emotionally relevant cues in females." (115)

THE REALITY OF RACE

Social constructivist orthodoxy has been more successful at shaping popular perceptions of race than of sex. As Murray notes, the idea that "gender is merely a social construct" is widely perceived as too extreme, but many of our contemporaries labor under the mistaken impression that "significant racial differences in cognitive repertoires are known to be scientifically impossible." (133)

Nevertheless, the author's discussion of race generously begins with a section entitled "What the Orthodoxy Gets Right." Richard Lewontin was correct that there is more variation within the major races than between them. Stephen Jay Gould was correct to criticize the theory of polygenesis, viz., that humans evolved independently in Europe, Asia and Africa for hundreds of thousands of years. No one today claims that races can be arranged in an unequivocal hierarchy from "best" to "worst." But all this merely means that "we have before us an exercise in modifying our understanding of race, not resurrecting nineteenth-century conceptions." (135)

In 2005, newly acquired data from the sequenced human genome confirmed that *Homo sapiens* originated in Africa; researchers found that "no origin outside Africa had the explanatory power of an origin anywhere within Africa." The circumstances of human dispersal from Africa are less clear. Some *Homo sapiens* seem to have been in the Mideast by about 200,000 years ago. It was long assumed there must have been many distinct migrations out of Africa, but evidence has recently emerged that today's non-Africans are mostly descended from a single small group:

> In 2016, a new whole-genome study based on 300 genomes from 142 diverse populations provided evidence for a one-wave scenario, indicating that just one band of anatomically modern emigrants from Africa has descendants among today's humans. But, as usual, there were complications. The genomes of Papuans gave signs that about 2 percent of their genomes might have come from an earlier population. That's not much, but it suggests something more complicated than a single band of emigrants. (147)

Some of the *Homo sapiens* of Eurasia mated with Neanderthals and Denisovans already there, acquiring useful genes in the process. As the population grew, bands would occasionally split off into new territory, resulting in stepwise increases in genetic drift and decreased genetic diversity; this is called "serial founder effect." The end result was a species in which differences in gene frequencies increased with distance and were subject to new evolutionary pressures across a wide variety of local environments.

As we know, there is no unequivocal number of human races. In such situations, it is helpful to run a *statistical cluster analysis*, in which a software program divides members of a sample first into two clusters, then three, increasing the number for "as long as the clusters produced continue to be informative." (149)

We now turn to the evidence for Murray's proposition five, viz., "Human populations are genetically distinctive in ways that correspond to self-identified race and ethnicity."

In 2002, a team of scholars associated with the Human Genome Diversity Project ran a cluster analysis on a sample of 1056 persons from 52 distinct populations, using 377 genetic variants. They found the cleanest set of clusters was produced when K — the number of clusters — was set to five, and that these clusters corresponded to the major continents: Africa, Europe, East Asia, the Americas and Oceania (the Pleistocene continent which included Australia, New Guinea and Tasmania). In general, genetic discontinuities are clearest where they correspond to geographic barriers.

Six years later, following the complete sequencing of the human genome, another group of scholars ran a cluster analysis on the same sample, but taking account of 642,690 variants rather than 377. Murray summarizes the results:

> At K = 2, two sets of the 51 populations had virtually no overlap: populations in sub-Saharan Africa versus populations in East Asia plus a few in the Americas. All the other populations were mixtures of the two clusters.
> At K=3, the people who showed virtually no admixture across clusters consisted of individuals from sub-Saharan Africa, today's Europe and Middle East, and the East Asian-Americas group.
> At K=4 the Amerindians split off to form a separate cluster.
> At K=5, the Oceania populations [=Australian Aborigines, New Guineans, Melanesians, and Micronesians] split off.
> At K=6, the Central and South Asians split off.
> At K=7, the configuration that the authors assessed as the most informative, those in the Mideast split off from the Europeans. (151)

Nota Bene: At no point does any increase in K fundamentally change the pattern of clusters; each increase splits one of the clusters already obtained, merely adding detail.

Murray draws our attention especially to the last two steps:

> As in the 2002 study, the first five clusters corresponded to the five continental ancestral populations ... [including] a cluster that corresponded to the classic definition of *Caucasian* — an odd agglomeration of peoples from Europe, North Africa, the Mideast, South Asia and parts of Central Asia. There had been a reason why physical anthropologists had once combined these disparate populations — all of them have morphological features in common — but it never made much sense to people who weren't physical anthropologists. With K = 7, one of the new clusters split off the peoples of the Mideast and North Africa and the other split off the people of Central and South Asia — precisely the groups that had always been visibly distinctive from Europeans and from each other in the Caucasian agglomeration. (152)

I am reminded of Steve Sailer's observation that Luigi Cavalli-Sforza's laboriously produced map of the world's "genetic population groups" resembles what Strom Thurmond might have sketched out with a box of crayons. In short, the common man's perceptions of the races of mankind turn out to be fairly well supported by cutting-edge genetic research.

Recent studies have focused on more fine-grained distinctions. For example, a 2016 review article showed

> what happens when several European subpopulations are plotted with different numbers of sites. When only 100 or even 1000 sites are used the subpopulations are indistinguishable. At 10,000 sites, some separation is visible. At 100,000 sites, Italians, Spanish, Germans, and Romanians are all reasonably distinct, with the British, Dutch, Swedish, and Irish fuzzily distinct. (154)

The upshot of these advances is that a geneticist can now say, in effect:

> Give me a large random sample of [genetic variants] in the human genome, and I will use a computer algorithm, blind to any other information about the subjects, that matches those subjects closely not just to their continental ancestral populations, but, if the sample is large enough, to subpopulations within continents that correspond to ethnicities.

As the author notes, "if race and ethnicity were nothing but social constructs, that would be impossible." (156)

Murray's proposition six states that "Evolutionary selection pressure since humans left Africa has been extensive and mostly local."

Indeed, the exodus from Africa accelerated evolution: not because mutations became any more common, but because new pressures were applied to pre-existing gene frequencies. For instance, the switch to a cooler Eurasian climate may have made certain previously neutral gene variants valuable, so that they spread within that local population (without necessarily reaching fixity). The transition to agriculture some ten thousand years ago led to a further series of drastic changes in human environments, generating intense new selective pressures and further accelerating evolution.

Before the sequencing of the human genome, researchers had to make educated guesses about where to look for genes recently subject to selection. Today, they can search the entire genome systematically in what are called "genome wide association studies." Even tiny changes in frequency at individual loci can have large cumulative effects over the whole genome. Geneticists have also developed methods for dating adaptations less than about 30,000 years old.

A 2016 review article summarized the results of 73 studies which have revealed recent adaptations affecting cell function, connective tissue development, the brain and central nervous system, vision, hearing, olfactory receptors, skin pigmentation, immunity and metabolism.

Such adaptations tend to be local, meaning (at a minimum) confined to particular continental races. A 2009 German study found that

> 68 percent of the regions [of the human genome] under selection were under selection for a single [continental] population. Another 20 percent were under selection in just two of the six. Only 1 percent were under selection in all six populations. (179)

This research is still at an early stage, and we will not know for a long time just how much recent evolution there has been in various geographical regions. But Stephen Jay Gould's claim that evolution since humans left Africa cannot have been extensive, while perhaps defensible when he made it in the 1980s, is now known to be mistaken.

Murray's seventh proposition states that "Continental population differences in variants associated with personality, abilities, and social behavior are common." Here is the evidence.

Research into continental differences in gene variants of all types is becoming more extensive in response to a growing awareness that diseases can affect different racial groups differently. This means that existing genomic data, collected mainly in Europe and the United States, may not be appropriate for use in medical research concerned with other parts of the world. Articles filled with fustian about "institutional racism" in medical science have even begun appearing in the popular press (if geneticists weren't "racist," they would presumably have been just as quick to collect samples from the deserts of Central Asia and the African jungle as in their own backyards).

Of course, this kerfuffle is having the positive result that genomic databases drawn from a wider array of racial groups are now being compiled. The goal is improved medical care around the world. But a side effect will be massive amounts of new data about racial differences in gene frequencies, many of which will correlate statistically with differences in personality, abilities and social behavior. *Human Diversity* provides information for 22 such traits for which evidence is already available (192–193). We cannot assume that all these differences have been produced by natural selection: founder effects and genetic drift probably made a larger contribution to some of them. But they are *real* racial differences in gene frequencies, whatever their cause.

As of yet, the task of assembling the genetic story for specific phenotypic traits has barely begun, but Murray assures us that "progress is accelerating nonlinearly" (201). By 2030, geneticists will be able to predict personality characteristics, abilities, and social behavior on the basis of genetic information alone, amounting to "an ironclad, you-can't-get-around-this-one refutation" (300) of social constructivism. The orthodox may still resist the evidence, but they will eventually succumb to the ridicule.

Human Diversity contains little on the genetic basis of racial differences in average intelligence; it is clear Murray never wants to be the subject of another moral panic like that which greeted *The Bell Curve*. He merely mentions that it is "tough" to defend the belief that "ethnic differences in IQ are meaningless," (206) and explains why in a long endnote (416–18). Here he points out that attributing the Black-White gap in America (or other Western countries) to "racism" predicts that Blacks would score higher in all-Black countries; in fact, scores are uniformly lower in Black Africa and Haiti than among for American Blacks. If you then appeal to "the legacy of colonial racism" (416), you must explain how colonialism affects IQ. The most plausible suggestion is through parental socio-economic status (SES). To test this hypothesis, one must adjust scores for parental SES. Murray notes that "this has been done frequently," and the literature "consistently shows that doing so diminishes the size of the B/W difference by about a third." In other words, two-thirds of the gap cannot be accounted for in this way. Moreover, most studies indicate that the B/W difference increases as parental SES rises; in other words, higher parental SES is associated with a rise in Black IQ, but with an even bigger rise in White IQ.

Other explanations offered for the race gap include Black's relative unfamiliarity with standard English, the administering of tests by white rather than by Black teachers, or Blacks' lack of motivation to work hard on tests which "clearly reflect White values." In response, Murray cites the consensus statement "Intelligence: Knowns and Unknowns" published in the February 1996 issue of the APA flagship journal *American Psychologist* in response to the public controversy surrounding *The Bell Curve*. The eleven experts reported that controlled experiments have revealed no substantial contribution to the racial gap from any of these causes (although they may play a role in particular cases). The statement also notes the high predictive value of tests for academic performance.

Since that statement was issued, experimental evidence has been produced indicating that the racial gap is "effectively eliminated" when Black and white students are "tested on the basis of newly learned information." The difficulty here is that such tests inherently measure short-term memory as much as, or more than, IQ; the gap disappears because the test is no longer so *g* loaded.

Murray acknowledges the possibility of arguing that the role of bias is too broad to be captured by any assessment of language and predictive ability. He calls this "the 'background radiation' theory of racism's effect on IQ." (418) This perspective interprets "racism" as an occult but omnipresent reality not unlike what Africans call "bad juju." As Murray says, such a perspective cannot be refuted with data, since it conceives of all data as vitiated *a priori* by racism; in other words, it is an unfalsifiable metaphysical commitment.

THE REALITY OF GENETIC INFLUENCES ON SOCIAL CLASS

More is known about the influence of genes on social class than upon race and sex; indeed, Murray writes that "the basics have been known for decades." (209) The technical literature treats socioeconomic status as the sum of heredity (genetic influence) and environmental influence. The latter component can be further divided into shared and nonshared environment. The nonshared environment includes things like birth order, differential parental treatment, extrafamilial networks, accidents and illnesses. Studying twins, especially monozygotic twins, is a useful technique for reducing the effects of the nonshared environment; usually such twins attend the same schools and have similar social circles. In practice, measurement error must be allowed for as well: e.g., the number of books in a child's home is one factor sometimes counted as part of its environment, but it is clearly a very imperfect proxy for how much intellectual stimulation the child actually receives in the home.

Hereditability, as it is understood in the technical literature, is "a ratio calculated as the variance attributable to genes divided by the total variance in phenotype." (210) It is a property of human groups, not individuals:

> Suppose that genes explain 70 percent of a population's variance in height. You can use this information to conclude that "genes

probably have a lot to do with how tall Joe is," but it does *not* mean that "genes explain 70 percent of how tall Joe is." (211)

Heredity is not a fixed number for any particular trait. For example, the heritability of IQ *rises* with age, a result many find counterintuitive. A child's IQ may be temporarily boosted, e.g., but over time the effect fades and the full effect of genes increasingly tells.

Heredity varies by population. For example, the heredity of SAT scores at an elite high school will be higher than at an ordinary school where the students have a wider range of abilities. This is easily understood if we bear in mind that heredity is a *ratio*: the narrower range of SAT scores at the elite school means that a smaller denominator is used for calculating that ratio.

The more environmental influences are equalized, the higher heredity becomes. As Murray explains:

> It is a statistical necessity: the phenotype is the result of genes and environment. In a perfect world where everyone had completely full opportunity to realize their talents, heritability of those talents would converge on 100 percent because the environment relevant to those talents would no longer vary. (212)

As early as 1976, two researchers noted that

> a consistent—though perplexing—pattern is emerging from the data. Environment carries substantial weight in determining personality—it appears to account for at least half the variance—but that environment is one for which twin pairs are correlated close to zero. We seem to see environmental effects that operate almost randomly. (219)

Or, as another researcher put it, "theories of socialization had assumed that children's environments are doled out on a family-by-family basis. In contrast, the point of nonshared environments is that environments are doled out on a child-by-child basis." (227) Accordingly, Murray's eighth proposition states: "The shared environment usually plays a minor role in explaining personality, abilities and social behavior."

In 2015, a group of seven scholars published a meta-analysis of nearly every twin study carried out between 1958 and 2012; it involved 2748 publications, 14,558,903 twin pairs, and explored 17,804 traits. From this enormous assemblage of data, Murray extracted the evidence on thirty traits relevant to personality, abilities and social behavior. Only for two of them was the contribution of the shared environment greater than one third: 36 percent for "basic personal interactions" and 34 percent for "problems related to upbringing." "Yes, these data seem to say, you can have some effect on your kids' manners and you can also cause problems." (223) For all 28 other traits, shared environment accounts for no more than 26 percent of variance. For such important traits as temperament and personality functions, work and employment, intimate relationships, and family relationships, shared environment contributes no more than 6 percent.

One must add the caveat that an extremely bad home environment can make a significant difference: i.e., truly awful parenting which involves severe deprivation and abuse *can* damage children permanently.

Wealthy parents can give their children a high standard of living. Often, they can get them out of youthful scrapes or into desirable first jobs. But, says Murray, "it's not so easy for parental influence to get the child promoted. The more competitive the industry and the more cognitively demanding the job, the less influence family wealth has." (221) And, of course, wealthy and high-status parents pass on to their children the genetic factors which partly explain their own wealth and success. What they *cannot* do is use their wealth or status to make their "children more than trivially 'better' than they would otherwise have been where 'better' is defined in terms of personality, abilities, or social behavior." (221)

Murray's ninth proposition states that "class structure is importantly based on differences in abilities that have a substantial genetic component." The basic reasoning behind this was set forth by psychologist Richard Herrnstein in 1973: 1) if differences in mental abilities are inherited, and 2) if success requires those abilities, and 3) if earnings and prestige depend upon success, then 4) social standing (which reflects earnings and prestige) will be based to some extent on inherited differences among people. This argument was set forth with 800 pages of detailed empirical support in *The Bell Curve*, a book cowritten by Herrnstein and Murray in 1994 and subtitled 'Intelligence and Class Structure in American Life.'

In the present work, Murray immediately follows up his ninth proposition with the following caveat:

> *The bulk of the variance in success in life is unexplained by either nature or nurture.* Researchers are lucky if they explain half of the variance in educational attainment with measures of abilities and socioeconomic

on in the human body all the time, but there does not seem to be any evidence that we will soon be able to control the process for our own ends. Murray warns that

> with rare exceptions, the mainstream media's reporting on the science behind epigenetics bears little resemblance to what's actually been discovered. (261) … As far as I can tell, no serious epigeneticist is prepared to defend the notion that we are on the verge of learning how to turn genes on and off and thereby alter behavioral traits in disadvantaged children (or anyone else). (268)

Murray points out that his final proposition, viz., that "outside interventions are inherently constrained in the effects they can have on personality, abilities, and social behavior," may not remain true forever.

> Who knows what role future drugs might play in enhancing learning and positively affecting personality traits and social behavior. At some point, the promise of … genetic editing will be realized, and all bets about the ability to change people by design in substantial numbers will be outdated. (269–270)

But we are not there yet.

IMPLICATIONS OF THE GENOMIC REVOLUTION

Human Diversity concludes with a consideration of the genomic revolution currently unfolding.

Older Americans learned about genetics in Mendelian terms where each gene coded for some trait which was normally either dominant or recessive. The genome as a whole was thought of as analogous to a large jigsaw puzzle. Once the entire genome was mapped, we could figure out which traits was encoded by which gene and the result would be a full understanding of inheritance.

Even long before completion of the human genome project in 2003, researchers began suspecting that things were going to get a bit more complicated this, both because some traits are under the control of more than one gene (polygenesis) and because some genes are associated with more than one trait (pleiotropy).

As recently as 1999, one of the pioneers of genome-wide analysis made news for suggesting autism might be under the control of fifteen or more genetic loci. That was thought to be an exceptionally high number at the time; today it is considered "quaintly low." (275) Since genome-wide analysis became possible, it has been discovered that, e.g., human height is caused by the combined effects of around 100,000 different loci. Indeed, statistical correlations with height can be measured for around 62 percent of *all* gene loci, although most of these probably have no causal effect. The word *omnigenic* has begun to appear in the literature. In short, Gregor Mendel got lucky with those pea plants of his back in the nineteenth century: he stumbled upon a monogenetic trait which simplified his interpretive task greatly.

As for pleiotropy, a 2018 study looked at correlations between genetic loci affecting general cognitive function and 52 health related traits. Statistically significant correlations were measured for no fewer than 36 of these, many of which had no obvious relations to cognitive functioning. Such results could soon become typical.

The notion of a straightforward correlation between traits and the genetic loci which "encode" them has, accordingly, been displaced by that of *polygenetic scores*. To measure a person's polygenetic score for a given trait, one must first know which single nucleotide polymorphisms (SNPs) are statistically correlated with that trait. Then one performs a genome-wide association study (GWAS) on the person. For each SNP, every human being inherits two alleles, one from each parent. Depending on which alleles the subject has, this yields a genotype score of 0, 1, or 2 for that SNP. These numbers are then added up for all statistically significant SNPs *as weighted by their statistical significance*. This gives researchers an estimate of how likely the individual is to exhibit the trait.

Polygenetic scores are useful to researchers because the causality runs in only one direction: personality, abilities and social behavior cannot cause polygenetic scores. Furthermore, they can predict from birth, even for late-onset phenotypes, and they have 100 percent test-retest reliability. They can also predict differences between family members, which twin studies cannot do. Polygenetic scores are normally distributed, meaning it will eventually be possible to measure means and standard deviations as we do with IQ and other normally distributed traits.

Medical research is the first domain where polygenetic scores have begun proving useful:

In 2010, two technical articles in the US National Library of Medicine contained the phrase "polygenetic score" or "polygenetic risk score" in the title or abstract. By 2015, that number was up to 47. In 2018, it was 171. (293)

But the effects of the new technique are unlikely to be limited to medicine. For example, behavioral geneticist Robert Plomin expects polygenetic scores to revolutionize psychology by allowing professionals to estimate the genetic risk patients have for disorders before they develop, for creating more precise treatments, and for shifting the focus from treatment to prevention.

Not everyone is equally impressed by the advance represented by polygenetic scores. The chief objection is that *statistical correlation is not causation*. A trait can be heritable in the statistical sense without having any genetic mechanism. For example:

> Marital status is highly heritable — 72 percent in one large-sample twin study. The heritability of divorce specifically has been estimated at around 50 percent. Because divorce is heritable, we can be sure that a GWAS will identify a large number of SNPs that are significantly associated with divorce. Suppose, for example, that some of the SNPs are related to the personality trait "irritability." Isn't that a plausible causal link to divorce? But we can't be sure even of that. Pervasive pleiotropy means the SNPs related to irritability are also related to a number of other traits that are just as plausibly a cause of divorce — or, conversely, might be related to resistance to divorce. Omnigenetics and pleiotropy work to create a causal map so sprawling and indeterminate that it is reasonable to conclude GWAS has taught us nothing new about the causes of divorce and finding more SNPs won't teach us anything important. (284)

In other words, as one critic of Plomin's claims has written: "Marriage and divorce are heritable, but they do not have a specific genetic etiology." (284)

More generally, the critics note that

> all complex human traits result from a combination of causes. If these causes interact, it is impossible to assign quantitative values to the fraction of a trait due to each, just as we cannot say how much of the area of a rectangle is due, separately, to each of its two dimensions. (285)

These critics are not merely expressing caution

about how many complications remain unresolved. They aren't just saying that it's early days yet and that we shouldn't get ahead of the data. They are saying that when it comes to complex traits, the GWA [genome wide association] enterprise is futile. (285)

Moreover, "complex traits" like divorce could be influenced by completely different genetically influenced traits in different people. Irritability likely makes one more likely to be divorced, but so does a propensity for philandering, and genes influenced one such trait may not be linked to the other. This reality has resulted in evolutionary psychologists emphasizing that the traits that should be studied are those for which there is evidence that they are directly under natural selection — traits like intelligence and the various personality systems.[1]

Insofar as science is about establishing causality, such skepticism about complex traits may well be correct. But, as Murray points out, a 'soft' science such as sociology "has never been about causal pathways and perhaps never will be. It's about explaining enough variance to make useful probabilistic statements." (286) For that purpose, polygenetic scores are going to be useful and thus, predicts Murray, will inevitably be used:

By the end of the 2020s, it will be widely accepted that quantitative studies of social behavior that don't use polygenetic scores usually aren't worth reading. (286) When large databases with genomic information are easily available, it will be akin to professional malpractice to conduct an analysis of social behavior that does not include genomic information. Few quantitative social scientists are going to write such analyses because they won't get past peer review. The question "Why didn't you take genetics into account?" will be universal and will have no good answer. (287)

Genome-wide complex trait analysis, or GCTA, is another new technique with uses and limitations similar to those of polygenetic scoring. These techniques are the principle reason for Murray's confidence that the days of enforced Lysenkoist orthodoxy are now numbered. He expects that genomic analysis will revolutionize physical anthropology, economics, political science and social policy as well as psychology and sociology, in part by permitting far more rigorous studies of environmental effects.

---

[1] Kevin MacDonald, "Cutting Nature at Its Joints: Toward an Evolutionarily Informed Theory of Conduct Disorder, *Journal of Social, Evolutionary, and Cultural Psychology* 6, no. 3 (2012): 260–291, 264.

However, such optimism may be misplaced given the pronounced leftist proclivities of much social science, particularly in highly politicized areas like sociology. Imagine the difficulty of publishing a study in a mainstream academic journal in which race is a variable and polygenetic scores are used for variables like criminality or intelligence.

CONCLUSION: WHY THE RESISTANCE TO BIOLOGICAL INFLUENCES?

In his final chapter, Murray reflects on the reasons behind the ferocity of our intellectual elite's devotion to social constructivist dogma. This is not a matter which can be decided by means of data and controlled experiments, of course; and by the same token, the empirical arguments of the previous chapters hold good regardless of what one thinks of Murray's remarks on this subject.

The premise concealed behind all the furious insistence on egalitarian dogma is a "conflation of intellectual ability and the professions it enables with human worth." The elites are smart, and smart people are strongly attached to their own intelligence and the things it enables them to do. Many of them imagine, therefore, that telling another group of people that nature gave them a lower average IQ is tantamount to a council of despair, as though this would make their lives less worth living. But this is not the way ordinary working people see matters.

As Murray notes, these natural differences were formerly discussed within the moral vocabulary of Christianity. God calls different men to different stations for reasons of his own — reasons that are inscrutable to human understanding; and it is rebellion against the Divine Will not to accept such providential arrangements. But our human value and eternal destiny are something else entirely: the king has no advantage over the peasant on the Day of Judgment. It behooves even the king, therefore, to retain a sense of humility and dependence on God's unearned grace.

Today's elite, having lost its Christian moorings, has lost any way of dealing with natural inequality. They seem to believe that high-IQ professionals are really "better" than working people in some fundamental sense, rather than simply more advantageously placed. In order for this situation not to outrage their moral sense, they must think of high status as something equally available to all at birth. Such a conception implies that they owe their own exalted abilities and status to personal effort, while their attitude "toward ordinary Americans is too often covertly condescending if they are people of color and openly disparaging if they are white." (316) Under their leadership, what Murray considers the four chief wellsprings of human flourishing—family, community, vocation, and faith—have largely dried up for the rest of society.

But the evidence presented in *Human Diversity* indicates that our cognitive and social elites are merely the winners of a genetic lottery. They stand in far greater need of humility concerning their own accomplishments than "disadvantaged minorities" do of social programs. As Murray notes, within living memory "it was considered un-American to be a snob, to look down on other Americans, and to think you were better than anyone else." Perhaps the most important consequence of the impending collapse of social constructivism will be the removal of an essential prop from the unbearable self-conceit of the Western elite. Then we can turn our attention to repairing some of the damage done on their watch to family, community, vocation and faith.

F. Roger Devlin, Ph.D., is the author of Alexandre Kojève and the Outcome of Modern Thought *and* Sexual Utopia in Power.

background. They're lucky if they can explain even a quarter of the variance in earned income with such measures. The takeaway for thinking about our futures as individuals is that we do not live in a deterministic world ruled by either genes or social background, let along by race or gender. But Proposition #9 is about social classes, not individuals. (228–229; emphasis in original)

Time and chance happen to us all, but they do not push us all in the same direction; spread over an entire society, the effect of genes will inevitably tell.

The general factor of intelligence, known as *g* and measured by IQ tests, is not only the most important heritable trait contributing to success, but far more important than any other individual trait. Recent confirmation comes from a study of 6653 UK twins which correlated scores on the British school-leaving exam known as the GCSE with nine heritable traits. IQ alone statistically explained 34 percent of variation, while the other eight combined explained just 28 percent.

In the US, criticism of testing has focused on the high correlation between parental SES and performance on college admissions tests such as the SAT. The big question concerns the direction of causation: is SES causing high scores, or is inherited intelligence what put these families in the high-SES category?

An exhaustive analysis of this question, along with a comprehensive review of previous studies was published in 2009 by a team of psychologists at the University of Minnesota. They found that controlling for admission test scores reduced the correlation of parental SES and college grades from +.22 to –.01. On the other hand, controlling for measures of parental SES only reduced the correlation between admission test score and grades only from +.53 to +.50. This would seem to leave little room for argument.

Evidence for the influence of IQ and parental SES on success in later life is less clear, but Murray cites thirteen measures based on six databases and in only two cases is the correlation coefficient for SES higher than that for IQ.

The final proposition states that "outside interventions are inherently constrained in the effects they can have on personality, abilities, and social behavior." In practice, 'outside interventions' usually refers to such practices as counseling, tutoring, mentoring, after-school activities and job training. The reasoning behind the proposition is simple: 1) if the shared environment explains little of the variance in cognitive repertoires (as stated in proposition eight), and 2) if the only environmental factors that can be affected by outside interventions are part of the shared environment, then 3) outside interventions are inherently constrained in the effects they can have on cognitive repertoires. In other words, "it is not within our power to do much to change personalities or abilities or social behaviors by design on a large scale."

The truth of this final proposition mostly follows from what has gone before, so rather than adducing evidence directly in its favor, Murray devotes his discussion to showing why five major objections fail. The first three dispute the first premise above, asserting that it is 1) wrong for some important outcomes, 2) wrong for the early stages of life, or 3) wrong when it comes to changing self-concept.

We saw that shared environment accounted for more than one third of variation for only two out of thirty traits related to personality, abilities and social behavior discussed in a thorough 2015 meta-analysis of twin studies. But there is no *a priori* cutoff for how much variation a factor must explain to be considered substantial. For six other traits, the shared environment accounted for over 20 percent of variation, including such important items as educational attainment (25 percent) and disorders due to multiple drug use (26 percent). If outside interventions could have an effect on the shared environment factor contributing to these traits, might they not be worth the effort?

The best-case scenario for improving shared environment is adoption:

> In effect, adoption at birth to competent parents gives us a glimpse of what would happen if an outside intervention could magically be successful at changing a wide variety of parenting behaviors from bad to good … . But adoption is as good as it gets. (246) If the shared environment explains just 26 percent of the variance, the outside intervention has to be big — boarding school, for example, or moving that family out of the neighborhood, or adoption into a new family. (242)

The sorts of outside interventions that can be applied to larger numbers of people later in life generally amount to no more than a few hours a week, and must compete against all sorts of other past and present influences. Social agencies simply do not have the means to apply more radical remedies on a large scale.

It is sometimes suggested that outside interventions can work in the early stages of life before habits have set and the child is more malleable. Murray acknowledges that

> if interventions are ever going to work, they're going to work in infancy and early childhood. But it's one thing to believe that; it's another to confront the empirical findings about the difficulties and constraints that have attended a half century of attempts to intervene early in life. (246)

When pre-school programs for disadvantaged youth were instituted in the 1960s, they produced a large effect: 35 percent of a standard deviation, nearly equivalent to half the Black-white kindergarten achievement gap. But subsequent experience showed this effect faded at a rate of 3 percent of a standard deviation per year. After 1980, even the initial effects of such interventions had shrunk to 16 percent, a finding which probably reflected improved conditions for children in the control groups.

In 1998, Congress mandated a large and rigorously designed evaluation of Head Start; the report was published in 2010.

> After one academic year in the program, effect sizes in six language and literacy areas ranged from .09 to .31 [i.e., 9–31 percent of a standard deviation], but there was negligible impact on math skills or on children's attention, antisocial or mental health problems. The limited effects at exit disappeared within two years. "By the end of the first grade, both achievement and behavioral ratings of treatment group children were essentially similar to control-group children." (251)

It is sometimes asserted that outside interventions can have a positive effect on a student's "self-concept." The original version of this theory led to the self-esteem movement, comprehensively de-bunked in the early 2000s. More recently, a somewhat more plausible variant has been put forward.

Researchers administered a Standard Progressive Matrices test to 5th graders. One group of children was praised for their intelligence, while another was praised for the effort they put into the test.

> Children praised for being intelligent subsequently displayed less task persistence and less task enjoyment. They became more

concerned about getting a good score than about learning new things. They became protective of their image as "smart" and reluctant to jeopardize it. (256)

As Murray wryly notes, this finding "was especially jarring for a society in which many upper-middle-class parents incessantly tell their children how smart they are." (256)

These findings have spawned the "growth mindset movement." Advocates believe an emphasis on intelligence is harmful because it teaches children that their results follow from a fixed trait. They strive to convey to students the efficacy of effort, teaching them to interpret failure as a stepping stone to later success.

Common sense suggests such an approach could be beneficial for at least some students, but empirical assessments of growth mindset interventions have yet to reveal large effect sizes. It is also difficult to disentangling the effects of the interventions from pre-existing personality characteristics such as openness and conscientiousness, as well as from cognitive ability.

A fourth objection to the constraints on outside interventions questions whether nonshared environment really cannot be affected by outside interventions.

The best way to study the nonshared environment is by looking at monozygotic twins reared together: they have the same genes and the same home environment, so differences must be due to the nonshared environment.

But it has been found that those differences are not stable over time. Cognitive differences last no more than a few years and personality differences change even more quickly. No identical twin differences are stable over many years. The necessary implication: the nonshared environmental factors are not stable, but more like random noise. (259–260)

Effective interventions, however, would have to be based on stable patterns.

The fifth objection is a recently fashionable appeal to "epigenetics." This is a relatively new field of study dealing with auxiliary mechanisms which switch off the expression of certain genes (by making them less accessible to transcription machinery), or in some cases switch them on or modulate the intensity of their expression. This is something which goes

THE OCCIDENTAL QUARTERLY

Western Perspectives on Man, Culture, and Politics

SUBSCRIPTIONS:

Students
(with copy of current student ID)
One Year: United States: $30, Canada: $40, Elsewhere: $50

Individuals
One Year: United States: $60, Canada: $80, Elsewhere: $100

Institutions
One Year: United States: $100, Canada: $110, Elsewhere: $150

Digital Version
One Year: Digital Downloads PDF format: $30

BACK ISSUES:

http://www.toqonline.com
Support: Support@theoccidentalquarterly.com

THE OCCIDENTAL QUARTERLY
P. O. Box 8127
Atlanta, GA 31106 USA

Editor: EditorTOQ@theoccidentalquarterly.com

Made in the USA
Columbia, SC
06 September 2020